I CHING

FOR BEGINNERS™

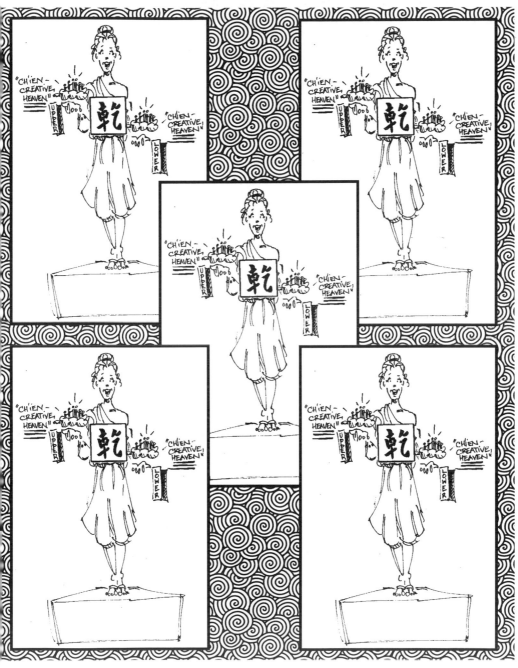

WRITERS AND READERS PUBLISHING, INC.

P.O. Box 461, Village Station
New York, NY 10014

Writers and Readers Limited
9 Cynthia Street
London N1 9JF
England
•

A Writers and Readers Documentary Comic Book
Copyright © 1996
ISBN # 0-86316-230-4 Trade
1 2 3 4 5 6 7 8 9 0

Manufactured in the United States of America

Beginners Documentary Comic Books are published by Writers and Readers Publishing, Inc. Its trademark, consisting of the words "For Beginners, Writers and Readers Documentary Comic Books" and the Writers and Readers logo, is registered in the U. S. Patent and Trademark Office and in other countries.

CONTENTS

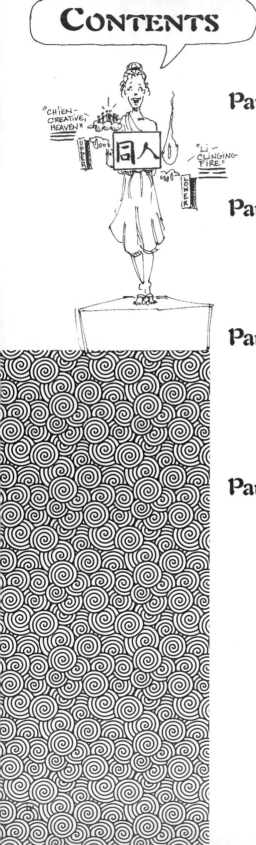

FOR BEGINNERS™

BY BRANDON TOROPOV

*"To every thing
there is a season..."*

PART ONE

Read This First

The I Ching, or Book of Changes, is one of the oldest books of wisdom, one of the Five Classics of Chinese literature, and one of the most influential books in human history. For nearly three thousand years, it has been held in the highest regard as a work of philosophy, an artistic achievement, and above all, an oracle.

The I Ching is based on the belief that random occurrences — chance occurrences — are not whimsical, accidental, or meaningless; but, on the contrary, chance occurrences are synchronized with some higher wisdom or universal order — if they are interpreted properly.

After thousands of years, people still consult the I Ching for guidance or advice or when seeking answers to important questions.

"ORACLE: an agency or medium that offers wise, authoritative, or highly regarded responses to an inquiry. Also: a person or thing serving as an agency of communication regarding the future."

1

But first, a bit of history...

Who "invented" the *I Ching*?

The *I Ching* is based on a system of eight "trigrams"—or three-line patterns (you'll learn all about trigrams in the next few pages). Most accounts credit the basic eight-trigram system at the core of the *I Ching* to the legendary Fu Hsi. This revered teacher is said to have formulated the trigrams after years of diligent study aimed at discovering nothing less than the principles governing all events in the universe.

According to most traditions, the essential text of the *I Ching* was developed later by King Wan and the Duke of Chou, Wan's son. Scholars believe that the king and his son expanded and combined the system of trigrams attributed to Fu Hsi and formalized the core of the book shortly before 1,000 B.C. There is every indication, though, that the oldest parts of

the work we now know as the *I Ching* have a chain of authorship stretching far earlier than that. The concepts and images attributed to King Wan and his son incorporate elements from other oracular systems, ancient poems, and historical works dating from centuries before they were born. The *I Ching*'s true origins extend into the deep recesses of ancient Chinese culture.

The *I Ching* underwent an expansion beginning in about the fifth century B.C., when an important series of commentaries on the main text were written and, eventually, appended to the main text. Although a good deal of (remarkably dry) scholarly debate has arisen over the authorship of these commentaries, known as the Ten Wings, many people attribute them, directly or indirectly, to the master sage Confucius, who was a devoted student of the oracle. Confucius, in his old age, is said to have remarked:

IF SOME YEARS WERE ADDED TO MY LIFE I WOULD GIVE FIFTY TO THE STUDY OF THE I CHING, AND MIGHT THEN ESCAPE FALLING INTO GREAT ERRORS.

HELLO MY NAME IS CONFUCIUS

Confucius's teachings and insights had an enormous influence on the development of the *I Ching* in China, and led it to greater popularity than ever as a tool for divination.

DURING the semibarbarous Chin dynasty (221-206 B.C.), Chinese literature suffered a terrible blow when a massive book burning destroyed most of the great written works of the culture.

The *I Ching* was one of the few significant writings to emerge intact from this catastrophe. As a result, scholars embraced the classic with great zeal, offering a wealth of commentaries from a variety of schools, including, most notably, the Taoists. During this time, and later, during the peaceful and creative Han dynasty (206-200 B.C.), the *I Ching* was used by many schools of thought — not only by the Confucianists — to offer insight into human events.

So — why is the *I Ching* so important now?

Although it is a product of ancient China, complete with oblique historical references reflecting the political struggles faced by King Wan and his son, the *I Ching* is fundamentally timeless. It relies on universal principles that have appealed to people in any number of social systems. The book's flexibility, and its general freedom from narrow dogmatic ideas, has no doubt had a good deal to do with its survival. Many other cultures have produced systems of divination; none of these systems, however, have had anything like the influence and longevity of the *I Ching*.

The book's core principle, although thoroughly Oriental, was later expounded by such Westerners as Carl Jung, who was fascinated by the work. Jung seems to have expressed the driving idea behind the *I Ching* when he discussed his own "synchronistic" view of the world we live in. Jung's theory of synchronicity offers a good entry point for Westerners seeking to learn about the *I Ching*, so we'll take a brief look at it here.

The idea of synchronicity has to do with what Westerners often think of as "simple chance" or "coincidence." As Jung saw it, any event that takes place at a given point in time may be identified, not only by its obvious — or "vertical" — causes, but by important shared linkages with other simultaneous events as well. These "horizontal" linkages are often overlooked in the noise and commotion of everyday life.

Put more simply, Jung realized that simultaneous events that appeared to have no causal connection could have meanings extending far beyond mere coincidence.

This is, in essence, the guiding concept behind the Book of Changes.

Jung's ideas about synchronicity, when considered alongside the texts and commentaries offered by the authors who composed the *I Ching* over a period of centuries, suggest something remarkable. They suggest that the answers to important questions can be found, not by isolating every possible logical connection to a problem, but by appealing to a set of observations selected under what most of us would probably consider a system of "simple chance." There's nothing otherworldly about the meaningful responses generated by such a method. In fact, many popular current books on problem-solving and creativity draw on very similar principles.

Using the *I Ching* has nothing to do with summoning spirits or calling on supernatural powers. Instead, it has to do with appealing to a system that took centuries to research and develop, contains profound insights about the human condition, and (most pragmatic of all) simply works well, for whatever reason.

The *I Ching* is the longest running show in town when it comes to finding meaningful answers to important questions.

What if I don't buy any of that?

You're in very good company. Any number of critics of oracles in general, and the *I Ching* in particular, find the idea of consulting tossed coins or yarrow stalks for information about the future to be logically absurd. They're probably right. In a way, absurdity is the intended starting point of the whole undertaking.

Logic, causality, and the use of human reason are all fine things, but sometimes they are not enough for a thorough and meaningful assessment of one's surroundings. The *I Ching* tends to view events in a way that undercuts traditional Western reasoning. It emphasizes full observation of the circumstances of the moment in question, without requiring strict logical explanations of what causes what. (A good Western analogue to this approach is the common advice to "think outside of the lines" in evaluating a difficult problem.)

As Jung, writing about the *I Ching*, put it,

WHILE THE WESTERN MIND CAREFULLY SIFTS, WEIGHTS, SELECTS, CLASSIFIES, ISOLATES, THE CHINESE PICTURE OF THE MOMENT ENCOMPASSES EVERYTHING DOWN TO THE MINUTEST NONSENSICAL DETAIL, BECAUSE ALL OF THE INGREDIENTS MAKE UP THE OBSERVED MOMENT.*

* Foreword to *The I Ching or Book of Changes*, Richard Wilhelm/Cary F. Baines, Princeton University Press, 1950.

As creative artists and problem-solvers can attest, the process of moving from an analytical mindset to a supremely observant one can be a joyous, liberating, and insightful experience. The sensation of being in touch somehow with the fundamental forces of the universe is a common, but difficult to express, reaction to that transition.

However their results are expressed in words, countless people find that the *I Ching* is one of the most tested and reliable tools yet devised for making that critical leap from analysis to presence and true understanding. A good number of the oracle's adherents (including the author) will not make any important future commitments or critical family or career decisions without consulting it.

Even after hearing such explanations, well-intentioned men and women have dismissed the *I Ching* as little more than a kind of parlor game. (This is actually an

understandable reaction, as the oracle is often invoked half-jokingly by people who have not yet learned exactly how to use it.) The beauty of the *I Ching*, however, is that it operates not only as an oracle, but also as a sublime work of literature that tells us a great deal about Oriental thought and, indeed, about the fundamental concerns of humanity. Because of this, even those who entertain serious doubts about the *I Ching*'s ability to "really tell the future" find exploring it worthwhile and illuminating.

What was all that about trigrams?

Trigrams (three-line patterns) and hexagrams (two-trigram patterns) are generated by tossing coins or yarrow stalks on a flat surface and recording the results. (In this book, we'll focus only on the coin-tossing technique, since it's a lot easier than the yarrow-stalk method.) Each trigram has a name, as does each hexagram. The images and meanings associated with the eight possible trigrams and sixty-four possible hexagrams, and the interpretation of those images and meanings, are the subject of the *I Ching*.

IF YOU USE ONLY THREE LINES AT A TIME, THERE ARE EIGHT WAYS TO ARRANGE PATTERNS OF SOLID AND BROKEN LINES. EACH THREE-LINE PATTERN IS CALLED A TRIGRAM. IF YOU PUT ONE ON TOP OF ANOTHER ONE, YOU CREATE A SIX-LINE PATTERN. THAT'S A HEXAGRAM.

We'll talk in more detail about trigrams and hexagrams a little later on in the book.

Is this book a replacement for the full text of the *I Ching*?

No. This book offers a brief accounting of the history of the oracle, a description of how to develop hexagrams, and a concise summary of each of the responses, as well as appropriate excerpts from the ancient texts. *The I Ching for Beginners* is intended as a starter book for those interested in consulting the *I Ching* on an informal basis. The complete work is one of humanity's profoundest accomplishments; one could spend a lifetime studying its innumerable complexities, and many very wise people have.

This book will yield insights and answers to the questions you pose to the oracle, but, for reasons of space, will not examine every line of commentary or every possible interpretation of the text. A starter book such as this one is probably essential for the newcomer, as the text and organization of the unabridged *I Ching* can be pretty intimidating in the early going. There are several reasons for this.

For one thing, the language of the book, even in a good translation, can be quite impenetrable; explanations about the historical context of some of the terms used are usually necessary. Accordingly, modern, reader-friendly explanations of some of the more baffling passages in the excerpted texts are provided here, as are summaries of the overall direction of each hexagram.

The advice in the I Ching is directed toward the kings of ancient China. The texts are a series of observations about the transitory nature of all human undertakings, and, more specifically, the best ways to instill good government in the face of political and social change. All the advice the I Ching offers is worthwhile, and you certainly don't have to be a king to use it, but as you read the judgments and commentaries you should probably consider yourself, for the sake of argument, to be a royal sovereign posing a question concerning sound administration of the kingdom.

Another problem: The unabridged book can be difficult to follow because the various layers of text — often centuries apart in composition — are not usually presented in an easily accessible sequence. *The I Ching for Beginners* offers a convenient hexagram-by-hexagram explanation of the sixty-four possible results, but it does not pretend to offer the final word on historical or textual issues that may be raised by such a grouping.

This book is meant to be incomplete. Its aim is to make you curious about the full text of the *I Ching*, which is just as worthy of sustained study as the books of the Bible or the plays of Shakespeare. After you've become familiar with the contents of *The I Ching for Beginners*, you may be inspired to move on to the full translation. (See the Bibliography for some suggested editions.)

Now, then — how do you build trigrams and hexagrams?

PART TWO

How to Throw and Read the Coins

The oldest (and most complicated) way to develop trigrams and hexagrams for use in consulting the *I Ching* is to throw fifty yarrow stalks and review the positions in which they fall. The most common method among Westerners, however, is the simpler one of throwing three coins, which is what we'll be focusing on here. Traditionally, Chinese coins, blank on one side and bearing an imprint on the other, are used; however, ordinary coins will serve just as reliably in eliciting responses from the oracle.

Our three coins, when thrown, can land in four possible combinations. ("Head" is regarded as the same as "blank"; "tail" is regarded as the same as "inscribed.")

1.	Head	Head	Head
2.	Tail	Tail	Tail
3.	Head	Tail	Tail
4.	Tail	Head	Head

Six throws are required. Each of the throws will result in one of the four combinations above, and each of these combinations is assigned a particular result that must be recorded. To understand the meaning of the results, however, a little background information is necessary.

When one consults the Book of Changes, one is asking for not one, but two hexagrams. (A hexagram, remember, is one three-line pattern, or trigram, on top of another.) The first hexagram offers an answer to the question at hand as it pertains to current circumstances; the second offers advice regarding future conditions. For example, one might ask, "What will happen if I quit my job?" The first hexagram will tell what you can expect as an immediate result of quitting, and the second will tell you what you can expect in the long term.

In posing your questions, you may want to start out by making them as specific as possible.

Ask, "What will take place if I press my partner for a long-term commitment?",

not "What's the deal with my relationship with Brenda?"

You should also avoid questions such as, "Should we buy the house we're considering, or wait until the real estate market improves?"

It's better to ask, "What will happen if we buy that house now?"

A LINE CAN BE BROKEN (IN WHICH CASE IT IS YIN, FEMININE) OR SOLID (IN WHICH CASE IT IS YANG, MASCULINE). HERE ARE THE LINE VALUES ASSIGNED TO THE FOUR POSSIBLE OUTCOMES OF TOSSING THE COINS:

YIN   YANG

1.	Head	Head	Head	Head — *Present:* solid [yang] line. *Future:* broken [yin] line.
2.	Tail	Tail	Tail	Tail — *Present:* broken [yin] line. *Future:* solid [yang] line.
3.	Head	Tail	Tail	Tail — *Present:* solid [yang] line. *Future:* solid [yang] line.
4.	Tail	Head	Head	Head — *Present:* broken [yin] line. *Future:* broken [yin] line.

To construct your two hexagrams, simply throw the coins six times, recording the results as you go in two columns — one for the present hexagram, and one for the future hexagram. (It is quite common to receive the same hexagram for both present and future.)

☞ *Important note:* Build your hexagrams from the bottom up!

The first coin you throw will yield the bottom-most lines; the second coin will yield the next lowest lines; and so on.

Thus, if you throw:

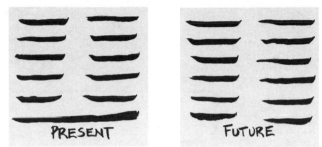

First throw:	Head	Head	Head
Second throw:	Tail	Head	Head
Third throw:	Tail	Head	Head
Fourth throw:	Tail	Head	Head
Fifth throw:	Tail	Head	Head
Sixth throw:	Tail	Head	Head

Your two hexagrams will look like this:

PRESENT   FUTURE

The only line that changes will be the bottom-most, or first, line. It will be solid in the present hexagram, and broken in the future hexagram.

There are any number of numerological issues that could be explored here about the reasons underlying this system. But this is a book for beginners, so we'll leave the complexities of the generation of yin and yang lines, old and young, changing and unchanging, for other books. Suffice to say, for now, that each answer one receives from the I Ching is twofold, and that each of the two hexagrams that result is composed of strong, masculine (yang) lines and/or yielding, feminine, (yin) lines.

THAT COVERS JUST ABOUT EVERYTHING!

Well, not really. Having thrown our coins six times, we've developed two hexagrams, each with an upper and a lower trigram. What happens next? What do the lines mean?

PART THREE

What the Trigrams Mean — and Where to Find the Hexagrams They Turn Into

As we've seen, the trigram, or three-line pattern, is the basic unit of the I Ching. There are eight trigrams, and sixty-four possible combinations of them.

Each trigram has a name and a set of specific associations that, when combined with another trigram, yields a hexagram with a particular meaning.

Here's a brief rundown of the eight trigrams, and some of the key associations that have been attached to each of them.

8 TRIGRAMS NO WAITING

CH'IEN — CREATIVE, HEAVEN, STRONG, FATHER —

K'UN — RECEPTIVE, EARTH, DEVOTED AND YIELDING, MOTHER —

CHEN — AROUSING, THUNDER, CAUSING MOTION, THE FIRST SON —

K'AN — ABYSMAL, WATER, DANGEROUS, — THE SECOND SON —

KEN — UNMOVING THE MOUNTAIN, RESTING, — THE THIRD SON —

SUN — GENTLE, WIND AND/OR WOOD PENETRATING, FIRST DAUGHTER —

LI — CLINGING, FIRE, GIVING LIGHT, SECOND — DAUGHTER —

TUI — DELIGHTED, MARSHES, JOYFUL, THIRD — DAUGHTER —

There are a host of other associations: directions, times of the year, parts of the body, even particular occupations and types of food. But the brief summary above is enough to give the main ideas underlying each trigram's function.

A hexagram, as we've seen, is made up of six lines. The top three lines are known as the upper primary trigram; the bottom three lines are known as the lower primary trigram. The interplay between these two trigrams, and the associations given to each, carry great influence on the meanings ascribed to each hexagram in the ancient texts.

In addition to its primary trigrams, a hexagram's nuclear trigrams were also important to the authors of the I Ching. Nuclear trigrams are those consisting of the second, third, and fourth lines (for the nuclear trigram in the position below) and third, fourth, and fifth lines (for the nuclear trigram in the position above).

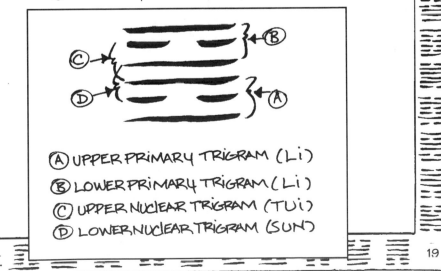

Ⓐ UPPER PRIMARY TRIGRAM (Li)
Ⓑ LOWER PRIMARY TRIGRAM (Li)
Ⓒ UPPER NUCLEAR TRIGRAM (TUi)
Ⓓ LOWER NUCLEAR TRIGRAM (SUN)

Analysis and discussion of a hexagram's primary and nuclear trigrams, and of its individual lines, are at the heart of the *I Ching*. The resulting discussions on points of conduct and right behavior constitute the substance of the oracle.

When you read good translations of the unabridged ancient texts that discuss the hexagrams directly, you will find, among other things, these critically important items:

① A Judgment. This is a brief, very old description of the import and theme of the hexagram in question. Although it makes a habit of using enigmatic language (you should get used to that), this part of the *I Ching* usually contains some reference to the hexagram's auspicious or inauspicious nature.

② An extended series of analyses of each individual line in the hexagram, rendered according to interpretations of very complex principles for determining auspicious and inauspicious placement of the yin and yang forces at particular points in the structure. These analyses serve as an opportunity to amplify the main message, and to offer specific examples and counter-examples that may (or may not) be appropriate to the reader's situation.

③ A commentary, usually clarifying its course of thought and offering specifics on the interpretation of the trigrams and of key lines. This material was composed later than either the Judgment or the original line-by-line analyses.

There's a great deal more to the hexagram-based texts, of course, but the three elements just cited are what are usually consulted by those appealing to the I Ching.

For the sake of simplicity, this book concerns itself primarily with the Judgment and the commentary on it, the first and third items listed above. The line-by-line analyses are important, but they are technically daunting and, thanks to their fondness for the poetic and occasionally paradoxical turn of phrase, prone to misinterpretation when applied by beginners to the situations they face. Once you've mastered the basic ideas covered in this book, you'll probably be ready to move on to an unabridged text for closer inspection of this part of the I Ching.

THE EXPLANATIONS OF HEXAGRAMS IN THIS BOOK FALL INTO TWO CATEGORIES: **THE MESSAGE** AND **THE MEANING**. IN **THE MESSAGE**, YOU'LL FIND A TRANSLATION OF THE JUDGMENT ON THE HEXAGRAM, FOLLOWED BY SOME MODERN-DAY EXPLANATORY MATERIAL THAT WILL HELP YOU MAKE SENSE OF THE JUDGMENT AND THE OVERALL STRUCTURE OF THE HEXAGRAM. THEN YOU'LL FIND A TRANSLATION OF ALL OR PART OF AN ANCIENT COMMENTARY ON THE JUDGMENT. IN **THE MEANING**, YOU'LL FIND A BRIEF, STRAIGHTFORWARD SUMMARY OF HOW YOU CAN APPLY THE IDEAS IN THE ANCIENT TEXTS TO THE SITUATION YOU FACE.

In THE MESSAGE, passages that have often been attributed to Confucius—or to members of his school—are marked with this symbol: ❖ These sections are usually worth reviewing closely.

In rendering the ancient texts, and as a starting-point in offering interpretations of them for modern readers, I have made use of James Legge's excellent 1899 translation of, and commentaries on, the *I Ching*, which appeared as the sixteenth volume in his *Sacred Books of the East* series. Where it has seemed appropriate, I have removed the occasional obsolete or outdated phrase from Legge and replaced it with one that would be more familiar to a contemporary audience.

Important note: Although it may be tempting to dive right into the book and pose questions, and although the book is certainly set up with ease of use in mind, I strongly recommend that you read the text from beginning to end before tossing the coins. Typically, a hexagram complements, in a special way, one that precedes or follows it, and the ancient sequence of the hexagrams is quite profound in and of itself. You'll get more out of The *I Ching for Beginners* if you familiarize yourself with the "landscape" of the oracle before you attempt to get a response.

Lets say I've thrown the coins and built the hexagrams. Then what do I do?

Identify the primary trigrams of each hexagram; use this table to find the number assigned to each one. Then turn to the appropriate hexagram in the main section of the book.

PRIMARY TRIGRAMS LOWER ↓ / UPPER →	CHIEN	KUN	CHEN	KAN	KEN	SUN	TUI	LI
CHIEN	1	11	34	5	26	9	43	14
KUN	12	2	16	8	23	20	45	35
CHEN	25	24	51	3	27	42	17	21
KAN	6	7	40	29	4	59	47	64
KEN	33	15	62	39	52	53	31	56
SUN	44	46	32	48	18	57	28	50
TUI	10	19	54	60	41	61	58	38
LI	13	36	55	63	22	37	49	30

~HEXAGRAM FINDING KEY~

A final thought: as you become more familiar with the *I Ching*, you'll come to see why it was named the *Book of Changes*. It is concerned, from its first word to its last, with the phenomenon of change in the conduct of human affairs, and with the correct responses to change in all its myriad forms. This ancient masterwork does not point the way toward an idealized state of being, or to some social or ideological construct that will succeed in weathering any assault time may make. It is, instead, informed throughout by the same wisdom that inspired the author of the famous lines from Ecclesiastes:

"To every thing there is a season, and a time to every purpose under heaven: a time to be born, and a time to die; a time to plant, and a time to pluck up that which is planted; a time to kill, and a time to heal; a time to break down, and a time to build up; a time to weep, and a time to laugh; a time to mourn, and a time to dance; a time to cast away stones, and a time to gather stones together; a time to embrace, and a time to refrain from embracing; a time to get, and a time to lose; a time to keep, and a time to cast away; a time to rend, and a time to sew; a time to keep silence, and a time to speak; a time to love, and a time to hate; a time of war, and a time of peace. What profit hath he that worketh in that wherein he laboreth? I have seen the travail, which God hath given to the sons of men to be exercised in it. He hath made every thing beautiful in his time: also he hath set the world in their heart, so that no man can find out the work that God maketh from the beginning to the end. I know that there is no good in them, but for a man to rejoice, and to do good in his life."

PART FOUR

The Hexagrams

In the closing years of Confucius's life, he became quite fond of the I Ching; it is said that he read his copy of it so much that he wore out three sets of the leather thongs that held the book's tablets together.

This section, which recounts some of the most basic interpretations of the sixty-four hexagrams, is the heart of *The I Ching for Beginners*; you'll know you've used it enough to move on to an unabridged version of the text when you feel as though you've mastered what follows. Don't worry; you haven't.

Hexagram One: Ch'ien
The creative

Primary trigrams: Chi'en — creative, heaven (upper); Chi'en — creative, heaven (lower).
Nuclear trigrams: Chi'en — creative, heaven (above); Chi'en — creative, heaven (below).

The message
The primary power is that which is great and originating, penetrating, advantageous, correct and firm.

❖❖❖

(Ch'ien is the name of the trigram representing heaven, creativity, and energy. In the human world, this hexagram, which incorporates Ch'ien in both the upper and lower positions, signifies the use of great, even elemental forces to attain correct ends. Ch'ien also carries the notion of continual movement and change. This hexagram, which focuses on ideas of time and transformation, performs a transformation of its own: its six unbroken [yang] lines yield naturally to the form-oriented, rather than energy-oriented, Hexagram Two. This reflects the idea that the creative power and the physical form in which it manifests itself are intricately connected.)

❖❖❖

❖ Vast is the primary power of the creative; all things owe to it their beginning. It contains all the meaning belonging to the name of heaven. The clouds move, and the rain is distributed; the various things appear in their developed form.

The method of the creative is to change and transform, so that everything obtains its correct nature, and great harmony is preserved in union.

The meaning
An auspicious situation. The realization of a suitable objective is attained through proper channeling of the primal forces of the universe. Using wisdom to tap into intense reservoirs of energy will cause unceasing movement and change, and the correct form will emerge. Summon your own deepest resources and take unyielding action; a continuous pattern of complementary actions will follow as a result. Not surprisingly, actions that reflect vanity, pride, arrogance, or self-satisfaction will result in the squandering of a great opportunity.

The creative force calls all things into being and serves as a guide to all events, but it does not assume control of a situation. By calling on your own true strength, and acting appropriately, you bring into play the strength of the universe.

Hexagram Two: K'un
The receptive

Primary trigrams: K'un — receptive, earth (upper); K'un — receptive, earth (lower).
Nuclear trigrams: K'un — receptive, earth (above); K'un — receptive, earth (below).

The message
The yielding power is that which is great and originating, penetrating, advantageous, correct and firm — with the firmness of a mare. When the exemplary one has to make any movement, the path will be lost unless the initiative is taken by another. Advantages: find friends in the southwest, lose friends in the northeast. When the exemplary one rests in correctness and firmness, there will be good fortune.

❖❖❖

(K'un is the name of the trigram representing earth; it appears both in the upper and lower positions here, generating a hexagram composed entirely of broken [yin] lines, and conveying a message of docility and subordination. This hexagram, which focuses on ideas of physical space and submission to duty, yields its own place by its very structure: its six broken [yin] lines change naturally to the energy-oriented, rather than form-oriented, Hexagram One. This reflects the idea that the creative power and the physical form in which it manifests itself are intricately connected. The directional references urge a yielding, yin approach: hexagrams associated with the southern and western directions are feminine in nature; those associated with the north and east are masculine.)

❖❖❖

❖ Complete is the great and originating capacity of the receptive. All things owe to it their birth; it receives obediently the influences of heaven. The receptive, in its largeness, contains all things. In its excellence, it is a complement to unlimited power. Its comprehension is wide, and its brilliance great.

The mare follows; she walks the paths of the earth and knows no boundary. She is mild and docile, advantageous and firm. Such is the course of the exemplary one.

The meaning
Beware of impatience or of heedless actions undertaken on impulse. Follow the directions of trusted associates or family members; do not commit yourself to a major change in the situation at hand on your own initiative. Quietly seek out assistance and follow the lead of others. Only by taking the subordinate position will the correct way be found.

Enlisting the aid of wise, capable allies is always good advice, but it is particularly important here. Follow the appropriate path to sound counsel, then yield to it after you have listened carefully. Find your strength in quietness and firmness, rather than rash action.

The exemplary one, supports all things by means of a great store of virtue.

GO WITH THE FLOW, JOE.

Key concepts:
Earth; form; yielding; gentleness; giving; obedience; femininity.

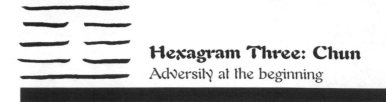

Hexagram Three: Chun
Adversity at the beginning

Primary trigrams: K'an — abysmal, water (upper); Chen — arousing, thunder (lower).
Nuclear trigrams: Ken — unmoving, mountains (above); K'un — receptive, earth (below).

The message
There will be great progress and success, and the advantage will come from being correct and firm, but any movement in advance should not be lightly undertaken. There will be advantage in appointing assistants.

❖❖❖

(Thunder rises, water descends. Chun shows how a plant struggles with difficulty out of the earth, rising gradually above the surface. This difficulty, marking the first stages in the growth of a plant, is used to symbolize the struggles that mark the emergence from a condition of disorder.)

❖❖❖

❖ The strong and the weak begin their interaction, and difficulties arise. Movement in the midst of danger gives rise to "great progress and success" through firm correctness. By the action of the thunder and rain, everything is filled up, but the time is one of disorder and obscurity.

Assistants should be appointed, but, having appointed them, one should not indulge in the notion that rest and peace have been secured.

The meaning
The new blossom emerges, and obstacles appear. Hazards and difficulties are to be expected; maintain a sound course in humble faith in the correctness of your cause, and you will persevere. When the storm passes, opportunities for favorable change will emerge. Valuable assistance from well-chosen subordinates may be essential to your undertaking.

Determination, commitment, and unfailing strength are required if one's early inability to cope with a chaotic environment is to be overcome. In time, troubles pass.

It is hard to remedy great disorder, but with faith in yourself and the destiny of your cause, this difficult task can be accomplished.

Key concepts:
Water; thunder; beginnings;
callowness; youth; inexperience;
undeveloped knowledge; lack of perception.

Hexagram Four: Meng

The folly of youth

Primary trigrams: Ken — unmoving, the mountain (upper); K'an — abysmal, water (lower).
Nuclear trigrams: K'un — receptive, earth (above); Chen — arousing, thunder (below).

The message

There will be progress and success. I do not go and seek the youthful and inexperienced one; instead, that person seeks me out. When the youthful one shows the sincerity that marks the first recourse to the oracle, I instruct him. If he asks a second or third time, that is troublesome, and I do not instruct the troublesome. There will be an advantage in being firm and correct.

❖❖❖

(A mountain with a dangerous, watery abyss below. One is advised to stop and consider the surroundings when faced with a dangerous situation! This hexagram sets out the method the exemplary one is to use in dealing with the inexperience and ignorance that may be encountered in an emerging state of affairs.)

❖❖❖

❖ A mountain, and below it a rugged defile with a stream in it. The conditions of danger and stopping.

It is a sacred endeavor to find what is correct in a fool and strengthen it.

The meaning

Water before the mountain; when there is fog, things do not emerge clearly at first. Something assumed as a fact may not represent the true state of affairs. However much this may frustrate you, it is important to retain your composure and act only after due consideration and reflection. Check every element of the problem before you; closely review every assumption you have made about the situation at hand.

The true nature of the situation becomes clear in time, but self-discipline and patience are essential if you hope to see it. Think twice before you reject the advice of an intelligent ally, and bear in mind that correcting yourself first is essential before you attempt to correct others.

Key concepts:
Mountains; water; fog; misapprehension;
initial ignorance; instruction.

Hexagram Five: Hsu
Waiting (Sustenance)

Primary trigrams: K'an — abysmal, water (upper); Ch'ien — creative, heaven (lower).
Nuclear trigrams: Li — clinging, fire (above); Tui — delighted, marshes (below)

The message
When one is sincere, light and success will appear. With firmness there will be good fortune; it will be advantageous to cross the great stream.

❖❖❖

(Danger, in the form of the K'an trigram, serves as an impediment to the creative, active force of Ch'ien, which suggests strength. Strength confronted by peril might be expected to advance boldly and initiate an immediate struggle, but the wiser approach is to wait until success is certain.)

❖❖❖

❖ To wait means to hold back. Danger in front; despite firmness and strength, one does not allow oneself to become involved with it. It is right not to be compelled or become overwrought.

"It will be advantageous to cross the great stream": Going forward will be followed by meritorious achievement.

The meaning
Clouds rise to the heavens; it will not be long before the rain falls and all is nourished by it. Attend faithfully and fully to responsibilities already undertaken, but show restraint with regard to your ultimate object. Await the proper time to act. Stay calm; gather your resources and build your strength. If you press ahead without considering the proper timing of your undertaking, you will meet with instant opposition and certain defeat. Focus your attentions on those aspects of your life that are most likely to endure, and you will remain free of error. Ultimately, you can attain your goal.

Bide the time; find the correct path; advance only when conditions are clearly to your advantage.

When waiting, it is essential to be deferential and to maintain the most disciplined self-control. if you do this, no harm will come to you.

Key concepts:
Water; heaven; patience, nourishment, light,
perseverance.

Hexagram Six: Sung
Conflict

Primary trigrams: Ch'ien — creative, heaven (upper); K'an — abysmal, water (lower).
Nuclear trigrams: Sun — gentle, wind (above); Li — clinging, fire (below)

The message

Although there is sincerity, one is nevertheless faced with opposition and obstruction. The one who stops in the middle is cautious and will meet with good fortune. Following all the way to the end brings misfortune. It will be advantageous to see the exemplary one; it will not be advantageous to cross the great stream.

❖❖❖

(The upper primary trigram, Ch'ien, provides strength and energy; the lower one, K'an, signifies peril. The idea is that of danger from without — and contention as the result. "Stopping in the middle" means resolving to withdraw from a hostile series of exchanges. This course is advised even if it entails a temporary setback. When one vows to pursue a certain obstructed course to the bitter end, one swears to proceed directly to the abyss. There is no point to hastening one's way toward obstruction and conflict.)

❖❖❖

❖ Danger and strength produce conflict. "Although there is sincerity, one is nevertheless faced with opposition and obstruction. The one who stops in the middle is cautious and will meet with good fortune": The strong has arrived, and occupies the central place.

"Following all the way to the end brings misfortune": Conflict is not a thing to be carried on permanently.

The meaning

Strength confronts you with peril, and conflict arises. It is not advantageous for you to fuel conflict; drop it and wait for better circumstances to emerge. Obstacles and obstructions await you; you must resist the temptation to commit yourself to opposing them. Anything you obtain by means of force may be taken away from you by means of force.

What will it gain you to follow an antagonistic episode to the bitter end? Leave off in the middle; abandon squabbling to those who feel compelled to squabble. Set your mind on the fundamental causes underlying your situation, and abandon thoughts of winning or losing.

The message here is clear and unmistakable; if you set yourself in strong opposition with the forces that await you, you will meet with misfortune.

Key concepts:
Strength; danger; perilous waters;
obstruction; caution.

Hexagram Seven: Shih
The Army

Primary trigrams: K'un — receptive, earth (upper); K'an — abysmal, water (lower).
Nuclear trigrams: K'un — receptive, earth (above); Chen — arousing, thunder (below)

The message
Give the army firmness and correctness, and a strong, experienced leader, and there will be good fortune with no error.

❖❖❖

(In the middle of the lower trigram, we find the only unbroken line in the figure. From this position arises the idea of a great general commanding the five broken (yin) lines. When conflict arises, civil disorder may follow. But generosity toward the people increases the ranks of the army.)

❖❖❖

❖ The army refers to a group of people; firmness and correctness refers to discipline. When one is able to use the people by instilling such discipline, one rises to the highest rank. The strong one who is in the center will elicit a response.

The people follow — there will be good fortune, and what error should there be?

The meaning
The earth sits atop water, a reversal of the natural order of things. In the situation at hand, you are likely to discover that harmony is lacking. Yet even in the face of change and contention, you will find that the correct path may be pursued. What is required is the steely determination and discipline of the general; work to instill these qualities in yourself, and you will find in due course that others are inspired by your example.

By taking the proper approach, which will incorporate both moral correctness and certainty of aim, you will be able to overcome all obstacles and attain a position of distinction.

Key concepts:
Earth; water; firmness; authority; danger;
dissension; devotion.

Hexagram Eight: Pi
Union

Primary trigrams: K'an — abysmal, water (upper); K'un — receptive, earth (lower).
Nuclear trigrams: Ken — unmoving, the mountain (above); K'un— receptive, earth (below)

The message

In union, good fortune results. But let one re-examine oneself, as though consulting an oracle, with regard to whether or not one's virtue is great, unremitting, and firm. If this is the case, there will be no error. Those who lack certainty eventually join; those who come too late will find that it goes ill for them.

❖❖❖

(Water sits atop the earth; when a river meets with the ground, it seeps in with the soil and becomes one with it. The harmony of union must be attained by a ruler or sovereign, and the necessary virtue appropriate to such an exalted position must be cultivated continually. In one sense, unity means distributing to others; society is in union as proper authority is passed along to others down the line.)

❖❖❖

❖ "In union, good fortune results": Union means mutual assistance. Inferiors follow along with docility. "Let one re-examine oneself, as though consulting an oracle, with regard to whether or not one's virtue is great, unremitting, and firm. If this is the case, there will be no error": All this follows from the position of the strong line in the center of the upper trigram. "Those who lack certainty eventually join": High and low will respond as appropriate.

Those who come too late will find that it goes ill with them": For them, the way has been exhausted.

The meaning

The water and the earth are in their natural and proper relationship, a propitious state of affairs. You are in an excellent position to strengthen alliances and solidify your position. Make common cause with the right people. Do not fall into the trap of forming partnerships with the wicked! Well planned cooperative efforts are particularly auspicious undertakings for you. Confidence from others and support from key people point you toward success. Do not delay your undertaking too long.

Yet the foundations supporting this favorable situation must be kept strong. Your own virtue is the all-important underlying factor that will allow you to take advantage of the favorable situation at hand. Do not be lulled into the delusion that occupying a place of authority and influence is a license for unreasonable or indulgent behavior.

The just ruler forms the proper alliances and encounters positive developments in the outside world. But that ruler knows that it is one's own sound heart that is the greatest determinant of true success.

In the old days, kings established the various states and maintained affectionate relationships with their princes.

Key concepts:
Water; earth; cooperation; sound relationships; alliance; unity.

Hexagram Nine: Hsiao Ch'u
The restraining power of the small

Primary trigrams: Sun — gentle, wind (upper); Ch'ien — creative, heaven (lower).
Nuclear trigrams: Li — clinging, fire (above); Tui — delighted, marshes (below)

The message
That which is small restrains and finds success. We see dense clouds, but no rain from the western border.

❖❖❖

(The single broken [yin] line occupies a critical position, and great forces are held in check. The yielding element, modest though it is, exercises influence for the time. Wind forces its way across heaven; the exemplary one refines the external elements of his being. If he were to persist at an inopportune time, misfortune would certainly arise. The reference to the lack of rain from the western border may be an obscure allusion to political conflicts involving a minor house that had attained a great deal of influence.)

❖❖❖

❖ That which yields holds the decisive position. Both those above and those below correspond.

Strength and flexibility. Strong lines are in the central places, and the will shall have free course.

The meaning
When your internal strength is combined with your carefully cultivated external gentleness, obstacles may be overcome . . . or, if need be, outlasted. The sense of this elusive hexagram is comparable to the advice in the Christian Bible to be "wise as serpents and gentle as doves." Although the situation at hand may incorporate its fair share of obstacles, the power of restraint and self-mastery is more than sufficient for you to prosper in due course. An attempt to force your way ahead in the face of an inauspicious set of circumstances is ill-considered. Steadfast development of character is a better course of action.

Avoid pessimism or ill thoughts. Even if events appear to take a turn for the worse, maintain faith in yourself and the forces that guide you. Do not lose yourself! Build an internal foundation of faith and trust for yourself, and resolve make constant improvements in the appearance you present to others. If you attend to both tasks, you will endure. If you try to press your luck in acting on a perceived advantage, or if you behave haughtily toward others, you will have cause to regret.

Key concepts:
Wind; heaven; patience; strength; yielding.

Hexagram Ten: Lu
Stepping

Primary trigrams: Ch'ien — creative, heaven (upper); Tui — delighted, marshes (lower).
Nuclear trigrams: Sun — gentle, wind (above); Li — clinging, fire (below)

The message
A foot set upon the tail of the tiger — and it does not bite! There will be progress and success.

❖❖❖

(The lower primary trigram indicates not only marshes, but also joy or satisfaction; placed below Ch'ien, the great symbol of strength, the hexagram expresses a favorable outcome in times of hazard. One emerges unhurt from danger; progress and success come about as a result of observance of all the rules of propriety. On these, as so many stepping-stones, one may step safely amid scenes of disorder and peril.)

❖❖❖

❖ Weakness stepping on strength. Pleasure and satisfaction, and response to that which indicates strength. Hence it is said, "A foot set upon the tail of the tiger — and it does not bite! There will be progress and success.

Possessed of strength, centrality, and complete correctness, one steps into the God-given position place and stays there with no error; one's light burns brightly.

The meaning
Right conduct, and attendance to the demands of form and propriety, carry the day. This hexagram reminds you to observe all due requirements when dealing with superiors, and to foster humility in your interactions with them. You should also be sure to show kindness and due forbearance to those who report to you. When you observe the right relations with others, anything is possible.

Cultivate the good will of important people; the situation at hand will respond better to efforts that have their blessing than to a rash initiative that is undertaken on your own. By all means, do not challenge or taunt a person in authority with your actions! Bear in mind that to step on a tiger's tail, you must be following it.

The exemplary one discriminates between high and low, and gives settlement to the aims of the people.

NOW THEN, IF I HAVEN'T SKIPPED ANY STEPS, I SHOULD HAVE ABOUT SIX MINUTES BEFORE THIS STARTS A THERMONUCLEAR REACTION...

Key concepts:
Sky; marshes; propriety; courtesy; purpose; degree; order.

Hexagram Eleven: T'ai
Peace

Primary trigrams: K'un — receptive, earth (upper); Ch'ien — creative, heaven (lower).
Nuclear trigrams: Chen — arousing, thunder (above); Tui — delighted, marshes (below)

The message
The small leaves, the great comes forward. There will be good fortune, with progress and success.

❖❖❖

(A course in which the primary forces are represented by the three strong lines, and the opposing forces by the three weak lines, must be progressive and successful. This hexagram is the polar opposite of Hexagram Twelve, Standing Still. In the present case, indications are of interrelation in all the correct places, and attendant growth and prosperity.)

❖❖❖

❖ That which is upper joins forces with that which is lower, and a single will prevails.
The way of the exemplary one appears increasing, and that of the inferior one decreasing.

The meaning
Three yielding (yin) lines are leaving; three strong (yang) lines approach. The situation is auspicious; things are progressing as they should, and your position is favorable. All aspects of the situation point toward union and a flourishing state of affairs. You may well have cause to celebrate something.

In dealing with others, focus on joining together. Address common goals. The result will be one that satisfies you. Both superiors and subordinates will benefit from assuming a single worthwhile objective.

Good people will rise to a position of influence and will help you to attain a worthwhile aim; those who sow trouble and division will lose influence. An excellent time for a new undertaking. Set your sights, then, on the proper goal, and pursue it with a calm spirit. The forces of good will come to your assistance if you renounce any claim to personal advantage, and act selflessly. If you are greedy, and grasp at things for your own gain, you will fall.

Act now; after fortunes ascend, they descend. When the period in discussion has run its course, there is no point in pretending that evil is not at the door.

Key concepts:
Earth; heaven; harmony; union; cooperation;
prosperity; beginnings.

Hexagram Twelve: P'i

Standing still (Stagnation)

Primary trigrams: Ch'ien — creative, heaven (upper)l K'un — receptive, earth (lower).
Nuclear trigrams: Sun — gentle, wind (above); Ken — unmoving, the mountain (below)

The message
Understanding between the members of the varying groups is lacking; indications are unfavorable for the perseverance of the exemplary one. The great leaves, the small moves forward.

❖❖❖

(A course in which the primary forces are represented by the three weak lines, and the opposing forces by the three strong lines, must be unhappy. This hexagram is the polar opposite of Hexagram Eleven, and as such it is not auspicious. In the present case, indications are of disharmony and tribulation. The time of growth is at an end; decay and deterioration follow.)

❖❖❖

❖ Earth fails to unite with heaven; all beings enter into disunion. That which is upper does not join forces with that which is lower, and the nation collapses. Weakness abides within, strength without; the inferior one abides within, the exemplary one without.

The path of the inferior one appears increasing, and that of the exemplary one decreasing.

The meaning
Three strong (yang) lines are leaving; three yielding (yin) lines approach. The situation is inauspicious; the wrong course has been taken, and toil, disharmony, and trial await you. The hexagram is strangely evocative of several famous lines from Yeats: things fall apart, and the worst people are full of passionate intensity. You may be separated from someone or something you love; you may face opposition from influential people of poor character.

A difficult, unlucky set or circumstances in all respects. How will you meet it? What, in other words, are you made of?

This is not the time to launch new initiatives. Wait for the wheel to turn; a period of severe trial must be borne with firmness, patience, and faith. After a time, distress and obstruction pass. If you keep to the correct path despite challenge and misfortune, you will find that a period of joy is approaching.

Heaven and earth fail to come into union; the exemplary one summons inner resources in order to find the way out of difficulties.

MOM WARNED ME THERE'D BE DAYS LIKE THIS...

Key concepts:
Heaven; earth; disharmony; disunion; lack of cooperation; lack of means; deterioration.

Hexagram Thirteen: T'ung Jen
Fellowship

Primary trigrams: Ch'ien — creative, heaven (upper); Li — clinging, fire (lower).
Nuclear trigrams: Ch'ien — creative, heaven, (above); Sun — gentle, wind (below)

The message
Out in the open area: progress and success. It will be advantageous to cross the great stream. It will be advantageous to maintain the firm correctness of the exemplary one.

❖❖❖

(The upper primary trigram is that of heaven, which is above; the lower primary trigram is that of fire, whose tendency is to rise upwards. Union is apparent, but it must be a union free from all selfish motives, and so the hexagram is placed in the open field, far from the depravity of the city. One brings about fellowship as the result of one's character, not because of the advantages conferred by a position in a hierarchy. Such fellowship will cope with the greatest difficulties, but caution and discretion are in order.)

❖❖❖

❖ "It will be advantageous to cross the great stream": The creative force sets forth and takes action. Harmony and a clear mind combine with strength, occupying the central, correct position, and corresponding properly to the surroundings. Such is the correct course of the exemplary one.

Only the exemplary one is capable of comprehending the minds of all who are beneath heaven.

The meaning
Fire mounts upwards, toward the heavens; things are headed in the proper direction. You are advised to undertake actions with others — but do so by pursuing the best possible aims, as identified by your own inner voice. Commit to a mutual advantage. Any hint of selfishness or pettiness may be enough to undermine your efforts.

Make common cause with others, and be sure your relationships with them are undertaken in the spirit of kinship and mutual support. If you do this without compromising yourself, and at the same time avoid falling into the trap of simply insisting repeatedly that you are in the right when disputes arise, you will reap a great benefit. Act wisely and temperately, bearing in mind the opinions of others; then success will come your way.

Key concepts:
Heaven; fire; coherence; union; victory in numbers; like-mindedness.

Hexagram Fourteen: Ta Yu

Possessing plenty

Primary trigrams: Li — clinging, fire (upper); Ch'ien — creative, heaven,

Nuclear trigrams: Tui — delighted, low-lying waters (above); Ch'ien — creative, heaven. (lower)

The message

There will be great progress and success.

❖❖❖

(The two primary trigrams, Li and Ch'ien, both rise; so do the two nuclear trigrams. Here, then, is a state of prosperity and abundance. What may endanger such a state of affairs? Only the pride it is likely to give rise to.)

❖❖❖

❖ That which yields occupies the place of honor, and is great in the center; things above and below respond. The name for this is "possession in great measure." Strength, firmness, order, and clarity are its attributes. It responds to heaven, and its action is at the proper time.

Thus, indications are for "great progress and success."

The meaning

Fire atop the heavens; all is clarified, evil is overcome, and the good is furthered. An unusually auspicious situation awaits you; you will find that the proper objective may be attained with relative ease. Your best qualities are magnified, and true dignity and virtue are in evidence in your actions. Your situation is likely to improve noticeably. This is a time of significant achievement and prosperity.

Great forces stand in full approval of your planned undertakings; they are ready to assist you. Do not do the powers that be the discourtesy of misusing their gifts or failing to act on the favorable situation before you.

This hexagram indicates, in an unusually straightforward and unenigmatic way, a very positive state of affairs for you.

The exemplary one overcomes that which is evil and encourages that which is good, and in so doing obeys the dictates of heaven.

YES, I SUPPOSE IT'S ALL RIGHT, AS OPENING ACTS GO...

Key concepts:
Fire; heaven; abundance; prosperity; rectitude; supreme good fortune.

Hexagram Fifteen: Ch'ien
Humility

Primary trigrams: K'un — receptive, earth (upper); Ken — unmoving, the mountain (lower).
Nuclear trigrams: Chen — arousing, thunder; K'an — abysmal, water (below)

The message
In humility, there will be progress and success. The exemplary one will conclude actions.

❖❖❖

(The previous hexagram having discussed the notion of great abundance, this one rightly delivers an important message concerning humility. The single whole (yang) line, in the third position, is strong, but humbles itself. The earth has been elevated.)

❖❖❖

❖ It is heaven's way to diminish the full and add to the store of the humble. It is earth's way to overthrow the full and replenish the humble. Gods and spirits inflict calamity on the full, and bestow blessings on the humble. It is humanity's way to to hate the full and love the humble.

Humility, when honored, spreads brilliance; when found in the low position, it cannot be ignored. This is how the exemplary one concludes actions.

The meaning
The lowly earth is set in a superior position; the strong line abases itself. Humility and modesty are your only ways toward lasting success. The circumstances facing you are auspicious if you do not engage in the folly of setting yourself above others.

The virtue of modesty, undertaken for its own sake, must serve as a counterbalance to any possible excesses on your part. If you follow this advice, you will attain success in your undertaking. By being willing to show honor and respect toward others, you will strengthen your character and show yourself worthy of the reward you seek. Remember that a humble person can still choose between wrong and right, and should be willing to stand up for the latter.

In general, you enjoy a favorable outlook. But bear in mind that all is dependent on your ability to show humility. The hexagram calls to mind a passage from the Christian Bible: "Blessed are the meek, for they shall inherit the earth."

The exemplary one takes away from that which is heavy and adds a little to that which is light; he weighs and measures and sets things into equality.

HEY, WAIT A MINUTE. I THOUGHT WE WERE ALL KNEELING FOR **YOU**.

ME? I THOUGHT WE WERE ALL KNEELING FOR **YOU**!

Key concepts:
Earth; the mountain; compensation; obedience; sincerity; generosity.

Hexagram Sixteen: Yu
Enthusiasm

Primary trigrams: Chen — arousing, thunder (upper); K'un — receptive, earth (lower).
Nuclear trigrams: K'an — abysmal, water (above); Ken — unmoving, the mountain (below)

The message

It is to one's advantage to set up princes as allies, and to put the troops in motion.

❖❖❖

(In the upper position, thunder and movement; in the lower, earth and obedience. Combining these ideas yields the notion of enthusiasm. The fourth line, which is undivided [yang], is regarded as the minister or chief officer of the ruler.)

❖❖❖

❖ The strong one is responded to; the instructions are carried out. Obedience summons movement, and the result is enthusiasm. Because obedience summons movement, heaven and earth accompany the effort. How much more appropriate it is, then, to set up princes as allies, and to put the troops in motion! Heaven and earth show docile obedience in motion; this is why neither the sun nor the moon lapse in their course, and why the sequence of the four seasons never fails. A holy person moves with obedience. Any penalty or punishment, then, is entirely just. Everyone obeys!

How great is that which the time of enthusiasm signifies!

The meaning

With thunder comes movement; the earth obeys. There are times when an objective for which you have prepared to struggle for some time is likely to be attained. This is such a time, but do not expect the opportunity to last forever. Take full precautions against misfortune, and then act boldly; success will be yours.

There is something to be said for cultivating subordinates who can be counted on to support your efforts; if you work with them to pursue a strong, well conceived plan, everyone will benefit. If, on the other hand, you are hasty or inattentive, you may learn a costly lesson. Even a hero knows how to lock the door at night.

Take the proper action, and bring every ounce of energy you have to the undertaking. You will be rewarded.

Key concepts:
Thunder; earth; groups; opportunity;
caution; preparation.

Hexagram Seventeen: Sui
Following

Primary trigrams: Tui — delighted, marshes (upper); Chen — arousing, thunder (lower).
Nuclear trigrams: Sun — gentle, wind (above); Ken — unmoving, the mountain (below)

The message
Great progress and supreme success. It will be advantageous to be firm and correct. There will be no error.

❖❖❖

(The arousing [thunder] obligingly takes its place beneath the joyous (the humble marsh). This gesture, taken together with the idea that the former trigram signifies the eldest son, while the latter signifies the youngest daughter, yields the images of following and submission. But the hexagram refers both the the act of following and the act of being followed, and it emphasizes the vital importance of pursuing correct action in either case.)

❖❖❖

❖ The strong comes and finds a place beneath the weak; there is motion and joy.There will be great progress and success, and, through firm correctness, no error. At such a time, everything under heaven will be seen to follow in one's path.

How great is that which the time of following signifies!

The meaning
The thunder humbles itself and assumes a low position, and a great benefit follows. Yield to the viewpoints of others, attend to their observations, be aware of their concerns — and your undertaking will be a success. Remember that the best leader is the one who knows when to follow! If you can bear this idea in mind, you will be in a position to enjoy very good times indeed.

Is there a course you should change as a result of the input or opinions of others? If so, attend to it carefully, and alter your destination. Those whom you may consider to be rivals could in fact be eager to assist you meet your goals. Win the assistance of others and you will be on your way to attaining an extraordinary benefit.

However, If you act heedlessly, ignoring those who offer sound counsel and worthwhile advice, you may come regret your actions bitterly.

Key concepts:
Marshes; thunder; listening; cooperation;
opportunity; counsel.

Hexagram Eighteen: Ku

Work on that which has fallen to disorder (Decay)

Primary trigrams: Ken — unmoving, the mountain (upper); Sun — gentle, wind (lower).

Nuclear trigrams: Chen — thunder, arousing (above); Tui — delighted, marshes (below)

The message

Supreme success. There will be advantage in crossing the great stream. Before the point at which it commences, three days; after the point at which it commences, three days.

❖❖❖

(Ku represents a state in which things are rotting or worm-ridden; the wind is blocked by the mountain, and in stagnant air there is often corruption. In this difficult hexagram we see the reversal of the decay, and a restoration to soundness that will lead to progress and success. Extraordinary effort is necessary to bring this reversal about; one must study closely the true causes of the initial corruption and act appropriately.)

❖❖❖

❖ The strong above, the weak below; pliancy and motionlessness: that which has fallen to disorder. To work on that which has fallen to disorder is to bring order into the world. "There will be advantage in crossing the great stream" — for the one who advances will encounter that which needs to be done. "Before the point at which it commences, three days; after the point at which it commences, three days" — for bringing beginnings out of endings is the procedure of heaven.

The meaning

In each ending is a beginning. The "three days" reference has to do with a Chinese calendar-name; the "point at which it commences" is the beginning of spring. What a difference three days in either direction can make!

You face a state of affairs that is unusually confused and complex, yet may also present extraordinary opportunity. The hexagram may point toward a serious organizational flaw, or toward deep-rooted family or marital problems. Nevertheless it holds out the promise of repair and reconciliation. Personal integrity and independence are of paramount importance if the work is to be done properly. After a time of healing, love and forbearance will pay handsome dividends.

Key concepts:
The mountain; wind; corruption;
disorder; illicitness; sickness; past errors;
reconciliation.

Hexagram Nineteen: Lin
Oversight of action

Primary trigrams: K'un — receptive, earth (upper); Tui — delighted, marshes (lower).
Nuclear trigrams: K'un — receptive, earth (above); Chen — arousing, thunder (below)

The message

There will be supreme success, and firm correctness will lead to an advantage. In the eighth month, mishap.

❖❖❖

(Lin, with its two strong (yang) lines advancing on four weak (yin) ones, provides an image of the onset and expansion of power and authority. The primary trigrams offer an image of earth placed above the marshes. The reference to the "eighth month" has to do with the months of the year assigned to this hexagram [in which the two strong lines advance], and the following one [in which the same lines retreat]).

❖❖❖

❖ Delighted and receptive; the strong is placed in the middle, and is responded to properly. There is great progress and success, along with firm correctness: this is the way of heaven. "In the eighth month, mishap" — before too long, a thing recedes.

The meaning

Strength and influence increase. The action you are about to undertake will be powerful and will be met with success. Force is not necessary; your efforts must be governed by a firm sense of what is right, and by a sense of caution. The advantage you hold is impressive, but it will not endure, so do not be seduced by it. Remember that everything we encounter in this life changes and passes in its turn. The situation at hand is nevertheless an auspicious one.

You're riding a wave that is on the rise; act appropriately, secure in your own virtue, and you will reach the heights for a time. While you are on the way up, be sure you share your benefits with others.

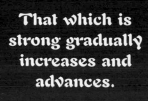

That which is strong gradually increases and advances.

BUT IT'S NOT FAIR. EVERYONE **ELSE** GETS TO WATCH NICKELODEON IF THEY FINISH THEIR HOMEWORK.

KID, YOU'VE CAUGHT ME IN A GOOD MOOD. GO AHEAD.

Key concepts:
Earth, marshes; ascent; increasing power;
moral strength; generosity; benevolence.

Hexagram Twenty: Kuan

Contemplating

Primary trigrams: Sun — gentle, wind (upper); K'un — receptive, earth (lower).

Nuclear trigrams: Ken — unmoving, the mountain (above); K'un — receptive, earth (below)

The message

The worshipper has washed the hands, but has not yet presented the offerings. Such a one is regarded reverently.

❖❖❖

(A great wind blows across the face of the earth. Before one advances in the face of such winds, one surveys the landscape. This hexagram symbolizes both the idea of showing and manifesting, and that of regarding or contemplating the situation at hand. The four weak [yin] lines look up in reverence to the two strong (yang) lines.)

❖❖❖

A great thing to be seen occupies an upper position. Docility and flexibility; here is one who holds a central position and a correct place, one for all the world to view.

The holy person lays down the instruction, and all who are under heaven yield.

The meaning

Maintaining the present position, and watching it carefully, is to be preferred over pursuing a new and uncharted course. It is quite possible that you are about to see a decline in fortunes. Postpone new initiatives for a time, and survey your situation (and that of your associates) carefully. You should be willing to accept proper instruction, no matter what form it takes. There is nothing to be ashamed of in stopping to take stock of where you are and what you are doing.

In time, important information may come to light; once you assess it properly, you will be in a better position to pursue your objective. With regard to the situation at hand, you will be well advised to take a moment to study closely the direction of the path you are traveling.

Key concepts:
Wind; earth; manifestation; showing;
watching; perception; observance.

Hexagram Twenty-one: Shih Ho

Biting past

Primary trigrams: Li — clinging, fire (upper); Chen — arousing, thunder (lower).
Nuclear trigrams: K'an — abysmal, water (above); Ken — unmoving, the mountain.

The message
Success. It is to one's advantage to see that the law is meted out.

❖❖❖

The odd name arises from the physical characteristics of the hexagram: the topmost line is the upper lip, the bottommost line is the lower lip, all the broken (yin) lines are teeth, and the remaining unbroken (yang) line is something being bitten. High and low must unite; that which separates the two jaws must be bitten through. The images of the hexagram are thunder and fire (or lightning), interpreted as the rule of law.

❖❖❖

❖ That which yields acts in a high position.

The place is less than appropriate, but it is to one's advantage to see that the law is meted out.

The meaning
Disparate forces remove the potentially dangerous obstacles to their union; high and low come together with complete understanding. Force or constraint may be necessary in some form if your goal is to be attained; just as a good judge can tell the difference between one who is guilty and one who is innocent, you must show firmness in the right cause. Often, this is a challenging task!

Good first principles, followed conscientiously, will carry the day over any obstacles you face. Your own rectitude and unflinching purpose will see you through. Bear in mind, however, that proper relationships with those of a different status must be maintained.

When you act in concert with others, you may take strong measures in defense of the righteous course that has been set out for you. Do not violate basic precepts, and your bold action will result in a favorable outcome. But disputes or troubles may beset you along the way.

Hexagram Twenty-two: Pi
Grace

Primary trigrams: Ken — unmoving, the mountain (upper); Li — clinging, fire (lower).
Nuclear trigrams: Chen — arousing, thunder (above); K'an — abysmal, water (below).

The message
Free course and success. It will be advantageous to undertake little things.

❖❖❖

(Pi combines clarity [in the lower position] with standstill [in the upper position]; the hexagram has to do with adornment, form, ornamentation, and decoration. Its basic idea is one of elegance and brightness, and its emphasis is on theoretical and artistic undertakings rather than practicality in the workaday sense of the word. The subject has nothing to do but to append adornments and attend to the true path, all from a humble position. But if the circumstances require change, every luxury and indulgence must be abandoned.)

❖❖❖

❖ We look at the form of heaven, and thereby ascertain the changes of the seasons.

We look at the form of society, and understand how the world is transformed.

The meaning
At night, the fire illuminates the mountain. There is nothing extravagant in this kind of display; that which is there is there. This is the most complete grace, and you should strive to emulate it.

The aspects of your immediate surroundings are relatively certain, but in extending your course beyond the borders of what is in front of you, you will probably be in for a few surprises. Your best course will be to keep your undertakings modest and on a scale you will be able to master.

Maintaining the proper form means arranging things in the right correspondence with one another. This may seem straightforward enough, but when one introduces many elements into the effort, a very complex undertaking indeed can result. In the present situation, you will

The exemplary one moves forward when the simple business of the day must be attended to, but controversial decisions are another matter.

LIKE THE OUTFIT? I BROUGHT SOME ACCESSORIES, TOO...

Key concepts:
Mountains; fire; adornment; beauty; sunsets; coherence; the arts.

Hexagram Twenty-three: Po
Splitting apart

Primary trigrams: Ken — unmoving, the mountain (upper); K'un — receptive, earth (lower).
Nuclear trigrams: K'un — receptive, earth (above). K'un — receptive, earth (below).

The message
It will not be advantageous to move in any direction whatsoever.

❖❖❖

(The solid [yang] force of the topmost line seems about to give way; beneath it, there is nothing but division. The mountain rests on the earth; how firm is the foundation? This hexagram explores the possible conditions that will allow one to endure in the face of extremely divisive forces.)

❖❖❖

❖ That which yields changes that which is strong. "It will not be advantageous to move in any direction whatsoever" — inferior ones rise in influence.

The exemplary one stops all forward movement, contemplates the figure at hand, and is cognizant of the way of change and alternation, whereby decrease is paired with increase, and fullness with emptiness.

The meaning
This seemingly inauspicious hexagram is actually a necessary, if sober, reminder of the changing nature of fortune, and an injunction to act appropriately in the face of challenge. Your position is subject to hazard from subversive forces, but the picture is not entirely bleak. If you summon up a strong sense of self and maintain your own source of wisdom at all times, you will avoid hasty or ill-conceived action and be able to respond appropriately.

A period of reflection, then, is in order. Don't make the mistake of procrastinating when it comes to examination of yourself and your circumstances.

Even if your position declines, there is no reason to abandon hope. Winter is followed by spring; night is succeeded by day; the moon wanes, and then begins to wax again. Your position, too, will improve in time, if only as a result of your deepened experience. The hexagram calls to mind the words of the prophet Isaiah: "In returning and rest shall ye be saved; in quietness and in confidence shall be your strength."

Key concepts:
The mountain; earth; division; challenge;
contemplation; endurance.

Hexagram Twenty-four: Fu
Returning (The turning point)

Primary trigrams: K'un — receptive, earth(upper); Chen — arousing, thunder (lower).

Nuclear trigrams: K'un — receptive, earth (above); K'un — receptive, earth (below).

The message

Free course and success. One finds no distress in one's exits and entrances. Friends approach, and no error is committed. One returns and retraces the way; in seven days, the return. There will be advantage in whatever direction movement is made.

❖❖❖

(Thunder within the earth; the first stirrings of great power. The forces described by this hexagram follow an unending course of movement and change; when decay has reached its climax, recovery can begin. Fu represents the month of the winter solstice, and as such describes a gradual return to influence of the forces of light. The "seven days" reference has to do with the re-emergence of the unbroken [yang] line after beginning to diminish in hexagram forty-four; the point at which, six changes later, there are no unbroken lines is found in hexagram two. This seventh hexagram marks the return of the yang force.)

❖❖❖

❖ That which is strong returns. There is motion and activity through the devoted; thus, "no distress in one's exits and entrances."

In returning, do we not see the mind of heaven and earth?

The meaning

The sustaining power moves back and forth, up and down; here, after a period of decline, its course begins a noticeable ascent. This is a time of rising fortunes.

An auspicious hexagram, particularly when it arises with regard to new undertakings, Fu suggests that you act with caution and tact, as the influence of the strong forces supporting you are only beginning to be felt. You are advised to get "back to basics" and to steadily pursue the right path without exhausting yourself. You will not regret doing so.

Your wheel turns, and a time of emerging benefit is the result.

In the old days, kings would mark the day of the winter solstice by shutting up their borders.

GOOD MORNING...

Key concepts:
Thunder; earth; approaching spring;
ascent; gradual improvement; reinforcement.

Hexagram Twenty-five:
Wu Wang
Innocence

Primary trigrams: Ch'ien — creative, heaven (upper); Li — arousing, thunder (lower).
Nuclear trigrams: Sun — gentle, wind (above); Ken — unmoving, the mountain (below).

The message
Great progress and success. There will be advantage in being firm and correct. If one is not correct, error results, and it will not be advantageous to move in any direction.

❖❖❖

(Beneath heaven, thunder sounds. Wu Wang describes an elemental, even primordial summoning of the life force, and in its earliest incarnation this force is entirely without cynicism, guile, or insincerity. For those who can act selflessly, in accordance with the dictates of this primary force, the way is open. For those with busy and contriving minds who seek advantage and the gratification of personal desire, ill fortune will result.)

❖❖❖

That which is strong comes from the outside, and is set up as the ruler on the inside.

When you do not possess innocence, where will you go? Can you do anything without the protecting force of the will of heaven?

The meaning
In the beginning, innocence is found. But what, exactly, is unexpected? Unfavorable developments from the outside. In the present situation, unusual adversity awaits you if you pursue selfish aims or take radical action.

In dealing with others, practice complete sincerity and honesty, of the kind that does not call attention to itself. Do not attempt to impose your will on your surroundings by insisting on pursuing the path you think is best; let things follow their own course, and you will do will. Natural forces will lead events to a successful conclusion.

You must avoid at all costs any rash, self-centered, or manipulative undertakings. If you indulge in impure ways of thinking and acting, you will encounter great misfortune.

The ancient kings made their regulations in complete accordance with the seasons, thereby nourishing all things.

SUMMON THAT ELEMENTAL LIFE FORCE, LADIES!

Key concepts:
Heaven; thunder; beginnings; passivity; naturalness; guilelessness; sincerity.

Hexagram Twenty-six: T'a Ch'u

The restraining power of the great

Primary trigrams: Ken — unmoving, the mountain; Ch'ien — creative, heaven (lower).

Nuclear trigrams: Chen — arousing, thunder (above); Tui — delighted, marshes (below).

The message

It will be advantageous to be firm and correct; if one avoids taking meals at home, there will be good fortune. It is to one's advantage to cross the great stream.

❖❖❖

(Heaven resides within the mountain; great things are stored up. This hexagram represents the ideas of restraint and accumulation; that which is repressed and restrained accumulates in strength and increases in volume. Ultimately, supreme virtue is cultivated. The reference to "meals at home" suggests that public service — and residence at court, rather than in a family dwelling — is to be pursued.)

❖❖❖

❖ Great strength, substantial solidity; these point toward a daily renewal of virtue. That which is strong is in the highest place; thus is seen the value set on talents and virtue. There is power to keep the strong in restraint.

The reason it is "to one's advantage to cross the great stream" is that heaven responds.

The meaning

Treasures reside within; what will you do with them? When you make a deposit, you should be sure you will earn interest on your money! Set about the cultivation of your own talents, and place unending emphasis on virtuous action and propriety. If you tend to the development of your own character, you will reap benefits and find yourself a position to undertake the most difficult enterprises. You will also enjoy support from influential quarters.

By storing up the great creative powers of the universe, you will show yourself as worthy. Actions undertaken for the general benefit of the public are particularly praiseworthy; do not dismiss such opportunities out of hand.

Learn from the experience and examples of others, and you will overcome immediate obstacles and find success in the long term.

Key concepts:
The mountain; heaven; stillness; creativity;
restraint; accumulation; virtue.

Hexagram Twenty-seven: I
The corners of the mouth
(Nourishment)

Primary trigrams: Ken — unmoving, the mountain (upper); Chen — arousing, thunder (lower).
Nuclear trigrams: K'un — receptive, earth (above); K'un — receptive, earth (below).

The message
With firm correctness there will be good fortune. We must look carefully at what we are seeking to nourish, and by the exercise of our thoughts seek the proper diet.

❖❖❖

(Thunder at the base of the mountain; movement takes place below that which is still, and we see the first evidence of life and activity. Taken together with the physical appearance of this hexagram [it looks like a mouth], we have the idea of nourishment. The nourishing may be of one's body, one's mind, oneself, or others.)

❖❖❖

❖ Heaven and earth nourish all things. Holy people nourish the talented and virtuous ones, and in this way reach the masses.
How great is the time of nourishment!

The meaning
The nourishment at issue in this auspicious hexagram may take many forms. You are the one who must choose what is to be sustained and nourished; if, in examining yourself and others, you follow an upright and correct path in choosing that which is to be encouraged and cultivated, you will encounter notable success.

The message may seem enigmatic, but it is actually quite profound. It recalls Shakespeare's observation on human nature: "Our bodies are our gardens, to the which our wills are gardeners; so that if we will plant nettles or sow lettuce, set hyssop and weed up tine, supply it with one gender of herbs or distract it with many, either to have it sterile with idleness or manur'd with industry — why, the power and corrigible authority of this lies in our wills."

Here you encounter notable opportunity. Choose that aspect of your own (or another's) character most worthy of nourishment, and it will lead you toward good fortune. Indulge the baser appetites, and you will regret doing so.

Key concepts:
The mountain; thunder; temperance; self-discipline; discretion; opportunity.

Hexagram Twenty-eight:
Ta Kuo

Exceeding in what is great

Primary trigrams: Tui — delighted, marshes (upper); Sun — gentle, wind (lower).
Nuclear trigrams: Chien — creative, heaven (above); Chien — creative, heaven (below)

The message
The beam sags, nearly to breaking. There will be advantage in moving in any direction whatsoever. There will be success.

❖❖❖

(In addition to symbolizing the wind, the Sun trigram represents wood — in this case, a single tree. Here, waters rise above the tree; the image is of solitude and confidence in renunciation. This is the course advised during times of exceptional turmoil or conflict. Through correct action, the sagging beam [indicated by the physical form of the hexagram] may be preserved.

❖❖❖

❖ The beam sags and nearly breaks, because there is weakness at the beginning and at the end. That which is strong is in preponderance and is positioned at the center. Flexibility and satisfaction lead to the conclusion that there is advantage in moving in any direction whatsoever, and then there will be success.

How truly great is the time of exceeding in what is great!

The meaning
The beam above you is about to snap! Extraordinary times require extraordinary measures. You may expect some difficulties, but if you maintain the proper mindset you may also expect circumstances favorable to overcoming those difficulties.

Stand tall and confident, then act. As a result of your inspired movement, an abnormal situation may be freed of all danger. Your own instinct in dealing with a challenging situation should be considered deeply. Act with caution and observe your surroundings carefully; if you do this and act appropriately, you will pass the test.

Let your actions be those called for by the exigency of the times, and not by whim or principle of your own. Then all will be well.

Key concepts:
Marshes or lakes; a tree; flexibility; caution;
extraordinary developments; renunciation;
solitude.

Hexagram Twenty-nine: K'an

Recurring hazards

Primary trigrams: K'an — the abysmal, water (upper); K'an — the abysmal, water (lower).
Nuclear trigrams: Ken — unmoving, the mountain (above); Chen — arousing, thunder (below).

The message

When one possesses sincerity, the mind penetrates. Correct action in such a situation will be of high value.

❖❖❖

(Water upon water. The meaning of the character K'an extends not only to water, but also to pits, dangerous caves, and the like. This character is strongly associated with danger. The hexagram at hand concerns itself with the question of how danger should be encountered, the effect it is likely to have on one's mind, and how best to get out of it.)

❖❖❖

❖ Water succeeds itself; one hazard follows another. This is the nature of water: it flows on, without accumulating its volume or overflowing; it pursues its way through a dangerous pass, without losing its true nature. It is said, "the mind penetrates" — for that which is strong is central. It is said, "correct action in such a situation will be of high value," and we see that advance will be followed by achievement.

Great indeed is the lesson concerning the season of danger!

The meaning

Like water at the lowest point, you find yourself in danger. Like water, you must be able to move appropriately without hesitation and without losing yourself. This is the best strategy if you wish to overcome danger.

Do not act heedlessly or without due consideration of your surroundings. The plain fact of the matter is that none of the options in evidence in the present situation are appealing, but you may, with patience and discernment, make your way to a better state of affairs. Hold firmly to the dictates of your heart, and follow the path you know to be right. Just as water flows constantly, so your own virtue must constantly be in evidence in your reactions to unfavorable events. Even in the face of adversity and peril, if you summon your deepest instincts, and act appropriately, you will learn from the situation and endure.

Key concepts:

Water; danger; decline; lack of direction or
bearing; caution.

Hexagram Thirty: Li
Fire

Primary trigrams: Li — clinging, fire (upper); Li — clinging, fire (lower).
Nuclear trigrams: Tui — delighted, low-lying waters (above); Sun — gentle, wind (below).

The message

It will be advantageous to be firm and correct, and thus there will be free course and success. Let the subject nourish a docility like that of the cow, and there will be good fortune.

❖❖❖

(Li is the name of the trigram representing fire and light, and the sun as the source of both of these. Its attribute is brightness, and, by a natural metaphor, intelligence.)

❖❖❖

❖ The sun and moon have their place in the sky. All the grains, grass, and trees have their place on the earth.

The double brightness of the two trigrams adheres to what is correct, and the result is the transforming and perfecting of all that is under the sky.

The meaning

One sun sets and another rises. Take advantage of an opportunity to express your creativity. Walk the right path, work on your humility, and listen to what others have to say, especially older associates. If you are offered advice, listen to it closely before rejecting it. There may well be something of value to you to consider.

Your work with others will be successful if you follow these admonitions. Avoid at all costs any rash, impulsive, or angry action. Look to the long term.

If you pursue your objective with a clear heart and do not waver from what is correct, your success is assured. If you attempt to cut corners, or if you otherwise persist on doing that which your conscience forbids, your effort will be doomed.

Key concepts:
Beauty; sunlight; shining brilliance;
intelligence; clinging.

Hexagram Thirty-one: Hsien
Courtship

Primary trigrams: Tui — delighted, marshes (upper); Ken — unmoving, the mountain (lower).
Nuclear trigrams: (above); Ch'ien — creative, heaven (upper); Sun — gentle, the wind (below).

The message
There will be free course and success. Advantageousness will depend on one's being firm and correct. In marrying a maiden, one encounters good fortune.

❖❖❖

(On the mountain, there is a lake; its waters yield to the mountain, and the mountain collects moisture from the clouds , thus replenishing the lake. A reciprocal relationship is described, one in which mutual influence is exercised. The two primary trigrams also signify young women (upper) and young men (lower); to grasp the hexagram's idea of selfless mutual influence, and the various ways such influence may be profitably bought to bear on a situation, it is good to recall that the power relationships set in balance by the marriage contract are of the highest importance. So harmony and good fortune may result from reciprocal spheres of influence.)

❖❖❖

❖ The weak above, the strong below; their two influences moving and responding to each other, and thereby forming a union. The male is placed below the female.

Holy people influence the minds of others, and the result is harmony and peace all under the sky; if we ponder the nature of influences, the true nature of heaven and earth, and of all beings, can be seen.

The meaning
Before choosing the right life partner, the correct relationship must be established. Similarly, you now face a situation in which exercising proper influence, correct in itself and for correct aims, is sure to be effective. Establishing the right position and the right terms for your undertaking will lead to good fortune and mutual benefit.

Yet the proper influence you must set into motion is undertaken utterly without selfish purpose; in fact, you may want to consider this type of influence as being without any purpose or motive whatsoever. Correct action and correspondence arise from your commitment to absolute readiness for any situation. That means keeping an open mind.

The exemplary one makes it easy for people to join his presence.

THIS IS ALL SO...SUDDEN...

DOES THIS MEAN I'LL GET WALKED MORE OFTEN?

Key concepts:
Lake; mountain; reciprocity; objectivity;
emptiness; correctness in mutual assistance.

Hexagram Thirty-two: Heng

Persisting

Primary trigrams: Chen — arousing, thunder (upper); Sun — gentle, wind (lower).

Nuclear trigrams: Tui — delighted, marshes (above); Ch'ien — creative, heaven (below).

The message

Successful progress and no error; the advantage will come from being firm and correct; movement in any direction whatever will be advantageous.

❖❖❖

(The previous hexagram used symbols associated with young men and young women and discussed wooing. In this one, the images of thunder and wind — in addition to relating that which is moving, penetrating, and therefore enduring — present the eldest son and eldest daughter. The idea is not of courtship, but of a long and stable marriage.)

❖❖❖

❖ Long continuance; the strong above and the weak below. Thunder and wind are in mutual communication, possessing the qualities of gentleness and movement. The strong and weak elements all respond to each other; in this way persisting is conveyed.

A holy person perseveres long in his course, and all things under the sky are transformed and perfect; if we ponder the things that give rise to persisting, the true nature of heaven and earth, and of all beings, can be seen.

The meaning

Thunder joins with wind and both endure; there is great power in persevering in doing the right thing. Your aim should be to take continuous, unceasing action on the path you know to be virtuous and correct. Continuously observe the duties you have conscientiously taken on, and all will be well.

This is not an invitation to rash action, but an injunction to stay the course you know in your heart to be correct. You must determine your proper role in the undertaking at hand, and act appropriately. If you do, good fortune will be yours. If it is your time to be submissive, do so without fail and in full faith of the correctness of your position. If it is your time to take the lead, assume responsibility without hesitation and see the task through.

Persevere along the correct path and you will reach your intended goal — and a new beginning.

The exemplary one stands his ground and never for a moment considers a change in course.

CALL ME ISAIAH....NAAH... CALL ME ISTANBUL.... NAAH...CALL ME LZZY. NAAH...

Key concepts:
Thunder; wind; perseverance; persistence; commitment; endurance; constancy.

Hexagram Thirty-three: Tun
Retreating

Primary trigrams: Ch'ien — creative, heaven (upper); Ken — unmoving, the mountain (lower).
Nuclear trigrams: Ch'ien — creative, heaven (above); Sun — gentle, wind (below).

The message

Progress and success. To a small extent, it will be advantageous to be firm and correct.

❖❖❖

(Heaven above, the mountain below; the two trigrams have been taken to represent superior and inferior individuals, respectively, with the former moving away from the latter. The general message of the hexagram is that small people may multiply and increase in power, thereby threatening the virtuous. At such a time superior individuals withdraw before their adversaries.)

❖❖❖

❖ Success is to be found in retreating. The strong is in the ruling place, and is properly responded to. One's action is in accordance with the times. "To a small extent, it will be advantageous to be firm and correct": there is encroaching and advancement.

Great indeed is the significance of the time that necessitates retreat!

The meaning

Heaven moves upward in the face of an accumulating power; the time for retreat is at hand. There are dark or unfavorable forces that rise in influence against you. Your success in minimizing the effects of such forces depends on your choice of when and where to retreat. Do not try to force matters; show persistence in modest instances of virtue and right action. If you act in this way, you will make the best accommodations possible.

You must accept the realities of the situation that confronts you. The threatening forces are on the increase, and there is nothing you can do about that. But by firm correct action, the resulting harm can be held to a minimum.

Do not confuse retreat with surrender. Your way is to maintain your objective, but to pursue it by sounder means than those you may be accustomed to. Keep people of low virtue and uncertain character at arm's length, if you must deal with them at all. Avoid picking fights with such people; simply maintain your internal strength with confidence and poise, and do what is necessary to keep them from exercising any negative influences.

Key concepts:
Heaven; the mountain; poise; strategic
withdrawal; persistence; endurance;
unfavorable forces.

Hexagram Thirty-four:
Ta Chuang

The power of the great

Primary trigrams: Chen — arousing, thunder (upper); Ch'ien — creative, heaven (lower).
Nuclear trigrams: Tui — delighted, marshes (above); Ch'ien — creative, heaven (below).

The message
It will be advantageous to be firm and correct.

❖❖❖

(Thunder resounds in the heavens; the expanding course of something quite powerful is in evidence. Yet strength alone is not enough if affairs are to be conducted successfully. Great power must be exercised with a firm sense of moral correctness if it is to result in favorable circumstances.)

❖❖❖

❖ That which is great is becoming strong. We see a situation in which strength directs movement; this is the essence of power . "It will be advantageous to be firm and correct": that which is great should be correct as well.

Greatness and correctness; the character and tendencies of heaven and earth can be seen in these.

The meaning
A thunderclap echoes in the heavens! You may be surprised at what it is in your power to accomplish; just be sure that your aim is virtuous and that you do not focus too much on yourself; after all, you are not the source of this power. Remember that the most powerful of all are the ones who exercise their influence selflessly, impartially, and for the good of all whom they affect.

Avoid at all costs any tendency toward intolerance or smugness. Exert your authority in harmony with that which you know to be morally sound, and do not seek to attain power for its own sake.

Use your strength to overcome any weakness in your own nature, and to carry out the best dictates of your will in your dealings with others. You will find that all doors open for you. If you attempt to use your talents in an unwholesome direction, however, you will find that the results are not conducive to either happiness or harmony.

This idea of power at one's disposal that increases to the extent that it is exercised for causes other than one's own is really not paradoxical at all. It complements the notion of selflessness laid down in any number of religious traditions, including Christianity: "Whosoever shall seek to save his life shall lose it; and whosoever shall lose his life shall preserve it."

Key concepts:
Thunder; the heavens; power, influence;
authority; self-restraint; propriety.

Hexagram Thirty-five: Chin
Moving Forward

Primary trigrams: Li — clinging, fire (upper); K'un receptive, earth (lower).
Nuclear trigrams: K'an — abysmal, water; Ken — unmoving, mountain (below).

The message
The prince secures tranquillity, and the king presents many horses to him. Three times in one day, he is received in person.

❖❖❖

(Above the earth: sunrise. That which enlightens rises over that which darkens. In this auspicious hexagram, rewards for worthy and virtuous action, actions that shine of their own accord like the sun, are bestowed.)

❖❖❖

❖ Clarity and brilliance above the earth; docile submission adheres to the great brightness; that which is weak advances and moves upward.

Taken together, these present the idea of "a prince who secures tranquillity, and the king presents many horses to him; *three times in one day, he is received in person.*"

The meaning
The sun ascends and virtue increases. The situation at hand is one in which it is your good fortune to be in the right place at the right time; actions undertaken are fruitful, and the result is auspicious. You may well find assistance and cooperation from people in powerful places.

This unusually favorable hexagram indicates a positive outcome in cooperative ventures, and the potential of great benefit for you when you undertake something that requires the help of an authority figure or benefactor. You should act to achieve your highest potential during this time of progress and expansion. Your own advantages and skills, firmly grounded in virtuous action, will rise to the occasion, almost of their own accord.

Yours is a position conducive to growth. Make the most of it.

Key concepts:
Sunrise; earth; shining brilliance; clarity;
accumulating virtue.

Hexagram Thirty-six: Ming I
Diminishing of the light

Primary trigrams: K'un — receptive, earth (upper); Li — clinging, fire (lower).
Nuclear trigrams: Chen — arousing, thunder (above); K'an — abysmal, water (below).

The message
During a time of difficulty, it will be advantageous to maintain firm correctness.

❖❖❖

(The light falls into the depths of the earth; the brilliance of virtue is obscured, but not blotted out. The situation is similar to that of an officer of the throne who must perform services for the sovereign, even though that sovereign is weak and lacking in perception — or perhaps even evil. In such a situation there is danger. The hexagram parallels several specific historic instances along these lines, outlined below.)

❖❖❖

❖ Brightness enters into the midst of the earth; the light darkens. Accomplished and bright within, pliant and submissive outside. The case of king Wan was that of one who possessed such qualities, yet met with great difficulties.

"During a time of difficulty, it will be advantageous to maintain firm correctness": — this has to do with obscuring one's own light, in the manner of one whose house and kin are beset with trouble, yet who maintains both aim and mind correct. Thus it was in the case of Prince Chi.

The meaning
Brightness is obscured and faced with serious obstacles. You are presented with an inauspicious situation — perhaps even betrayal on the part of those close to you. You must beware of the influence of those in authority whose aims are not virtuous, or whose lack of skill in leadership may carry dire consequences for you and others. Only steely discipline and rigorous effort on your part will offer you the possibility of enduring in such difficult circumstances. Your internal light must shine, even if it is hidden for a time.

The first task is to acknowledge that you face a time of hardship and great challenge. After you have done this, the only sensible course is to reinforce those elements of your own character you know to be virtuous. Although the situation at hand may carry its share of unpleasant moments, you must nevertheless be resolute, and perhaps even show some sly creativity, in your attempts to find the correct response to unfortunate events. When issues of survival or great obstruction arise, a certain quiet inventiveness — inventiveness that might, in less demanding times, be considered craftiness — may be in order.

The light is obscured by the earth; thus the exemplary one conducts his management of others, showing intelligence by keeping it obscured.

WHEN HE SAID HE WANTED THE KEYS TO THE BULLDOZER, DID YOU ASK HIM WHAT HE WANTED TO DO WITH IT?

WELL, NO...

Key concepts:
Earth; light; repression; obstruction; misfortune; honor; resolve.

Hexagram Thirty-seven: Chia Jen

Members of the family

Primary trigrams: Sun — gentle, wind (upper); Li — clinging, fire (lower).
Nuclear trigrams: Li — clinging, fire (above); K'an — abysmal, water (below).

The message
What is most advantageous is that the woman be firm and correct.

❖❖❖

(Wind issues from fire; similarly, the order and harmony that issues from the family unit brings coherence to the larger world. Although the hexagram points toward domestic harmony, it is also an essay on the stability that arises when each member of a group performs the appropriate tasks. This hexagram takes the family as the basic component of the state.)

❖❖❖

❖ The woman has her correct place inside, the man has his correct place outside. That man and woman occupy their correct places is the great righteousness shown in heaven and earth. In a family, there are those who rule with authority, namely the parents. Let the father be the father, the son the son; let the elder brother be the elder brother and the younger brother the younger brother; let the husband be the husband, and let the wife be the wife. Then the house is well.

Bring the house to a condition of order, and all under heaven and earth will be established.

The meaning
Don't be thrown by the seeming emphasis on gender stereotyping here; you are in a position of great opportunity, and with harmony and proper attendance to duty, you can attain your objective. Work hard and do not be distracted. Through cooperation with others and focus on the proper division of labor for the task at hand, there will be a time of great flourishing.

Regulating the actions of others in a complex undertaking first requires that you know your own proper place in the group. Even if that position is not one of leadership, you will find that correct attendance to its requirements is the first step to notable success.

Good cooperative work requires that you accord a measure of respect to each of your companions, and that you avoid acting impulsively. Do these things, and then do your best, and all will be well.

Key concepts:
Wind; fire; family; harmony; balance;
propriety; adherence to structure.

Hexagram Thirty-eight: K'uie

Opposition

Primary trigrams: Li — clinging, fire (upper); Tui — Delighted, marshes (lower).
Nuclear trigrams: K'an — abysmal, water (above); Li — clinging, fire (below).

The message
In small matters, there will be success.

❖❖❖

(Fire burns upward, water flows downward; the two directions give rise to disharmony. The hexagram describes a social state in which division and mutual alienation prevail, and offers advice for achieving the modest remedies possible in such a situation.)

❖❖❖

❖ Two sisters live together, but their wills do not move in the same direction. Harmonious satisfaction is attached to bright intelligence; the weak advances and acts above, occupying the central place and being responded to by the strong. This is why there will be "in small matters, success."

Heaven and earth are separate and apart, but the work they do is the same. Male and female are separate and apart, but with a common will they seek the same object. There is diversity between the myriad classes of beings, but there is a great underlying analogy between their various activities.

Great indeed are the results of this condition of opposition.

The meaning
The house is not in harmony; you should not expect the easy accomplishment of any major goals. But you must remember that the period of conflict and separation of interests that faces you is the natural outcome of the situation you have entered; this time of disunion will pass, and will yield its place to a more harmonious period.

You should strive to seek common ground and keep your goals modest. Complications will undoubtedly arise, but your reaction to them must be one of strength and equanimity. Act virtuously at all times, do not yield to the temptation to cut corners or abuse alliances, and beware of trusting people too far.

As you face the upcoming challenges, bear in mind that opposition is a necessary precursor to unity. This difficult period can be, must be, endured and transcended. There is a Buddhist notion of an intricate, wholly compelling delusion that suggests our separateness from others — and another of the necessity of ultimately awaking from that vivid hallucination. Both ideas are appropriate here.

The exemplary one admits diversity even when there is general agreement.

WHAT THIS HORSE DOESN'T SEEM TO REALIZE IS THAT HE AND I ARE, IN ACTUALITY, ONE AND THE SAME ENTITY...

Key concepts:
Fire; marshes; disunity; alienation; division; disagreement.

Hexagram Thirty-nine: Chien

Barriers

Primary trigrams: K'an — abysmal, water (upper); Ken — unmoving, the mountain (lower).
Nuclear trigrams: Li — clinging, fire (above); K'an — abysmal, water (below).

The message

Advantage is found in the southwest, and not found in the northeast. It will be advantageous to meet with the great one. With firmness and correctness, there will be good fortune.

❖❖❖

(Water is restrained at the top of the mountain; it cannot follow its natural course, because the boulders of the summit prevent it from doing so. The hexagram deals with the best way to proceed when faced with obstruction, impediment, or possible crippling injury. Because the north is associated with danger, and the northeast with mountains, the safe path is identified as the southwest; the main idea behind the directional references is the vital importance of selecting a path that will lead to safety.)

❖❖❖

❖ Difficulty. There is peril ahead. When one sees the peril and can stop in place, one is wise.

"Advantage is found in the southwest" because one advances and takes the central place, and "not found in the northwest" because the pathway stops. That "it will be advantageous to meet the great one" suggests that advance will lead to achievement. There is an appropriate place, and "there will be good fortune," for the regions of the kingdom are brought to order.

Great indeed is the work to be done in the time of obstruction.

The meaning

The water will overcome the limitations imposed on it when it accumulates enough to flow over the rocks. Similarly, you must attend to the development of your true self during times of limitation and danger. By raising your own character to its highest level, you will find the strength to overcome the obstructions that face you. Know where you are; seek help as required; sustain your own virtue.

At some times, action on your part will be appropriate; at other times, inaction will be appropriate. Distinguishing between the two situations is the business of wise people, and your own wisdom in dealing with the present situation may well need to be augmented. This is the message of the present cautionary, and occasionally enigmatic, hexagram.

Chien does clearly indicate, however, that a certain healthy wariness before moving ahead will be well advised on your part. The assistance of elders or senior advisers will probably be helpful in determining your next action.

Key concepts:
Water; the mountain; blockage; danger; dilemmas; caution; dangerous pathways.

Hexagram Forty: Hsieh
Release

Primary trigrams: Chen — arousing, thunder (upper); K'an — abysmal, water (lower).
Nuclear trigrams: K'an — abysmal, water (above); Li — clinging, fire (below).

The message
Advantage will be found in the southwest. If no further operations are called for, there will be good fortune in returning. If some operations are called for, there will be good fortune in concluding them as early as possible.

❖❖❖

(Thunder and rain; the cleansing effect of a great thunderstorm is suggested. The hexagram concerns itself with the idea of loosening pent-up forces or untying that which is bound. The reference to "the southwest" suggests a successful path—see the previous hexagram.)

❖❖❖

❖ Peril results in movement. By moving, one finds an escape from the peril. This is the meaning of release. At a time of release, "advantage will be found In the southwest": one moves and wins over the many. There will be good fortune in returning": such an action wins the center. "If some operations are called for, there will be good fortune in conducting them as early as possible": such operations will be successful.

When heaven and earth are freed, we have thunder and rain. when these come, the buds of the plants and trees that produce the various fruits begin to burst.

Great indeed are the signs of the time of release.

The meaning
A cloudburst, and the air is cleared. After a long period of adversity and obstruction, the great pathway is opened to you. This is the perfect time to reach out and seize opportunity.

Conflicts, misunderstandings, legal disputes, and transgressions all recede in influence. This is a good time to forgive old wrongs. You face in the current situation a time of growth and advancement in fortunes. The only obstacle you may encounter is that of failing to initiate prompt, aggressive action toward a worthy goal. Take advantage of the auspicious circumstances you face. Do not hesitate; a beautiful day doesn't last forever.

The exemplary one offers clemency to those who have erred, and forgiveness to evildoers.

I CAN SEE CLEARLY NOW...

Key concepts:
Thunder; rain; spring; growth; joy; vitality; dispersal.

Hexagram Forty-one: Sun
Reduction

Primary trigrams: Ken — unmoving, the mountain (upper); Tui — delighted, marshes (lower).
Nuclear trigrams: K'un — receptive, earth (above); Chen — arousing, thunder (below).

The message
If there is sincerity, reduction will lead to great good fortune: freedom from error; firmness and correctness that can be maintained; and advantage in every movement that shall be made. How shall this be undertaken? In sacrifice, two baskets of grain may be presented.

❖❖❖

(Marshes situated at the foot of the mountain; the waters evaporate and nourish the vegetation above. The theme is one of diminution in order to aid some higher purpose, the diminishment and curbing of all that is in excess. The hexagram's physical structure supports this idea: the image is seen as that of a lower trigram made up of all solid [yang] lines generously "donating" its top line to an upper trigram made up entirely of broken [yin] lines. The reference to "baskets of grain" suggests that even a modest offering may be appropriate to fulfill the obligation in question.)

❖❖❖

❖ The lower is diminished, and the upper is expanded. The route describes an upward motion. "Two baskets" suggests a fitness with the time.

There is a time when the strong should be diminished and the weak should be strengthened — as, indeed, diminution and increase, overflowing and emptiness all take place in harmony with the conditions of the time.

The meaning
The marshes yield their moisture to the mountain; there is a time of reduction and loss, yet the loss results in new life. The situation you face is one in which attendance to your own excesses is of the utmost importance. If you can check that part of yourself not in accordance with the right, you will act appropriately. The costs you incur may be high or low, but they must be appropriate to the situation.

Show sincerity in your efforts at self-discipline, and you will enjoy great rewards. Even if the correction — or some contribution towards it — is very small, it will be accepted as appropriate to the time if it is heartfelt and represents your best effort. The emphasis of this difficult hexagram is not so much on good or ill fortune, but on the continuous effort required to build strong character and avoid errors arising from intemperance.

Key concepts:
The mountain; marshes; sacrifice; restraint; self-control; discipline; attendance to that which is in excess.

Hexagram Forty-two: I
Increase

Primary trigrams: Sun — gentle, wind (upper); Chen — arousing, thunder (lower).
Nuclear trigrams: Ken — unmoving, the mountain (above); K'un — receptive, earth (below).

The message
There will be advantage in every movement that is undertaken; it will be advantageous to cross the great stream.

❖❖❖

(Wind above, thunder below; during a storm, each helps to strengthen the other. From this comes the idea of growth, reinforcement, and increase. The physical structure of this hexagram — in which the upper trigram "donates" one of its unbroken [yang] lines so that the lower trigram may be reinforced — is also reminiscent of the idea of increase. The upper trigram symbolizes not only wind, but also the wood from which a boat may be fashioned.)

❖❖❖

The upper is diminished, and the lower is expanded. The satisfaction of the people is without limit. That which descends from above reaches all who are below, and the course is great and brilliant.

"There will be advantage in every movement that is undertaken": this appears from the centrality and correctness of one's position. There is blessedness.

Increase shows movement and docility, and there is daily advancement to an unlimited extent. Heaven dispenses and earth produces, leading to increase without restriction.

Everything having to do with increase takes place according to the requirements of the time.

The meaning
Reinforcement and increase; good times, perhaps even a windfall. When you come across the possibility of great bounty, it is incumbent upon you to ensure that others may share in it when it arrives.

Indications are that you will be successful in your undertakings, and that you are in a position to overcome even the greatest difficulties. Bear in mind that the only true advantage you will enjoy during a time of prosperity is that you will be entitled to see to it that the benefits you encounter are distributed as broadly as possible.

Act vigorously to open up the path, and your efforts will be successful. But your exploits must never be selfish; they must always be undertaken to improve the state of those around you.

Key concepts:
Wind; thunder; reinforcement; addition;
augmentation; abundance; gain.

Hexagram Forty-three
Kuai
Displacing

Primary trigrams: Tui — delighted, marshes (upper); Ch'ien — creative, heaven (lower).
Nuclear trigrams: Chien creative, heaven (above); Chien creative, heaven (below).

The message
A full accounting of the circumstances must be made in the royal court, with due honesty and sincerity. There is peril. One should also make an announcement in one's own city. Recourse to arms is not advantageous. There will be advantage in whatever one goes forward to.

❖❖❖

(The waters of the marsh have evaporated, and have ascended, in the form of clouds, to the heavens. A cloudburst is likely. This hexagram examines the means at one's disposal for avoiding tempests of a political and social nature, and the upheaval associated with such tempests. Specifically, this hexagram addresses the problem of dealing with the inferior person — symbolized by the top line — who comes to a position of great influence and opposes a virtuous regime. It strongly suggests that the virtuous party will carry the day.)

❖❖❖

❖ That which is strong displaces that which is weak. Strength and delight lead to displacement, but harmony continues.

"A full accounting of the circumstances must be made in the royal court": the weak rests on five strong lines. "Honesty and sincerity" entail peril — but such peril that, when confronted directly, leads to brilliance. "One should also make an announcement in one's own city. Recourse to arms is not advantageous": what such a man exalts soon exhausts itself.

"There will be advantage in whatever one goes forward to," because the strong grows and increases to a point of completion — and brings an end to the matter.

The meaning
Clouds break open and skies threaten. You must take a stand with regard to people of poor character who occupy positions of power.

Ignoring those who wield power poorly won't serve your purposes; neither will confronting them directly on their own terms. You must meet the challenge through the force of your own character, and by winning the hearts of those who can help you to bring about positive change. Setting out — for or a virtuous person in high authority — the specific details of the misdeeds that concern you may yield good results; so may encouraging public sympathy for your cause. But the most important step is to maintain firm faith in the correctness of your undertaking, and to observe moderation in all your dealings with others. Personal grudges must not motivate your actions.

Key concepts:
Marshes; heaven; threatening skies;
corruption; virtue; resolve.

Hexagram Forty-four: Kou
Encountering

Primary trigrams: Ch'ien — creative, heaven (upper); Sun — gentle, wind (lower).
Nuclear trigrams: Ch'ien — creative, heaven (above); Ch'ien — creative, heaven (below).

The message
A powerful woman. Best not to marry such a woman.

❖❖❖

(One attribute of the lower trigram, representing wind, is penetration; the upper trigram, representing the creative force, also signifies royalty here. The hexagram's images lead to the idea of a prince's instructions being disseminated successfully throughout the realm. The single broken [yin] line at the bottom signifies a less-than-virtuous power trying — in vain — to establish a foothold in the kingdom. Those of inferior character are compared to a poor marriage prospect.)

❖❖❖

❖ An encounter; the weak encounters the strong. "Best not to try to marry such a woman": one cannot make a long-term match with her. Heaven and earth meet together, and the entire natural world is displayed. That which is strong finds itself in the central and correct position; all things under heaven prosper.

How great is the significance of what has to be done at the time of encountering!

The meaning
The winds scatter the royal commands to the four corners of heaven; thankfully, such a positive influence is more than sufficient to ward off the influence of inferior people. You should take care in the selection of subordinates or partners, and should monitor closely the influence of those who report to you or work with you. There may be trouble afoot.

Although the positive influence at work in your affairs has been countered by a negative force, that negative force is not, in the current situation, powerful enough to take root . . . unless you neglect it and allow it to flourish.

Do not allow people of poor character to be entrusted with too much responsibility. If you permit them to exert their influence, they will turn others to their way of thinking, and cause a gradual decline in your fortunes. Rapid action will address this problem and allow you to avert a downturn. Inaction or rationalization, on the other hand, will mean that the destructive forces will take root and grow.

Even a puny little pig may come in time to stamp around in a great rage.

OK, MAYBE HE **WASN'T** THE BEST ASSISTANT I COULD HAVE TRACKED DOWN.

Key concepts:
Wind; heaven; pernicious influences;
corruption; encroachment.

Hexagram Forty-five: Ts'ui
Gathering

Primary trigrams: Tui — delighted, marshes (upper); K'un — receptive, earth (lower).

Nuclear trigrams: Sun — gentle, wind (above); Ken — unmoving, the mountain (below).

The message
The king repairs to his ancestral temple. It will be advantageous to meet with the great man; then there will be progress and success, though the advantage must come through firm correctness. The use of great offerings will lead to good fortune; in whatever direction movement is made, there will be advantage.

❖❖❖

(The marshes are set above the earth; to keep its waters from being dispersed, it yields to the restraining influence of the banks.. The upper hexagram carries the meaning of happiness, and the lower that of receptive obedience. The image as a whole is an auspicious one indicating a contented multitude. The king's return to the ancestral temple suggests an extremely favorable encounter with great powers.)

❖❖❖

❖ Obedience and satisfaction. The strong occupies the central place. Others gather in a mass around that point. "The king repairs to his ancestral temple": a pious and reverent gesture. "It will be advantageous to meet with the great man; then there will be progress and success": the resulting union will be thoroughly correct. "The use of great offerings will lead to good fortune; in whatever direction movement is made, there will be advantage": all is done in accordance with the ordinances of heaven.

When we look at the way in which the gathering together takes place, we behold the true conditions of heaven and earth, and of all things.

The meaning
The marshes are restrained by the earth; a period of unity is at hand, and wisdom dictates that steps should be taken to preserve such conditions. You should make the most of this opportune time, and should, at the same time, be on your guard against threats from envious outsiders and malcontents within.

This is a time when you may expect to avail yourself of great personal and material resources. Do not underestimate the value of sound counsel from elders and senior officials in your efforts to make the most of this prosperous time.

With due caution concerning the influence of divisive people, and with the cooperation of others, you can expect to enjoy a bountiful harvest.

Key concepts:
Marshes; earth; unity; prosperity;
boundaries; order; happiness; obedience.

Hexagram Forty-six: Sheng

Pushing up

Primary trigrams: K'un — receptive, earth (upper); Sun — gentle, wind (lower).

Nuclear trigrams: Chen — arousing, thunder (above); Tui — delighted, marshes (below).

The message

Great progress and success. Seeking to meet with the great man, one needs not fear. Advance to the south will be fortunate.

❖❖❖

(In addition to representing wind, the lower trigram also denotes wood; the image is interpreted here as that of wood growing upward from within the earth. A sapling's slow, steady persistence in the face of the obstacles that surround it is a good reminder of the central idea of this hexagram. The "south" is the region of brightness and warmth; advancing toward it signifies joyful progress.)

❖❖❖

❖ The weak finds the opportunity and ascends upwards. Flexibility and obedience; the strong below and the proper correlate above. These things indicate that there will be "great progress and success."

"Seeking to meet with the great man, one needs not fear": there will be reason for congratulation.

"Advance to the south will be fortunate": one's aim is carried out.

The meaning

Trees do not grow in an instant, but slowly; similarly, your fortunes are gradually improving. You may expect, with good effort and attendance to seemingly minor developments of virtue in your character, to rise to the highest pinnacle of distinction, and to overcome any obstacles that stand between you and your goal.

There is an expression, "Till by the square inch, and the whole field will yield a good harvest." It is appropriate for you to bear in mind here. By attending properly to the smallest matters, your upward movement is maintained.

A contemporary Zen story tells of a teacher who asked a carpenter how the renovations to the Zen center were coming along. "Very nearly done," the carpenter replied. "Just a few details left to take care of." The teacher looked at him quizzically. "'Just a few details?'" the teacher asked. "What else is there besides details?"

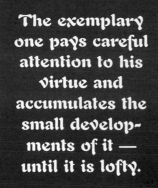

The exemplary one pays careful attention to his virtue and accumulates the small develop- ments of it — until it is lofty.

HEY, IS IT MY IMAGINATION, OR HAVE YOU PUT ON A LITTLE HEIGHT?

THANKS FOR NOTICING.

Key concepts:
Earth; wood; growth; fertility; patience;
attentiveness; accumulating virtue; progress.

Hexagram Forty-seven: K'un

Exhaustion

Primary trigrams: Tui — delighted, marshes (upper); K'an — abysmal, water (lower).
Nuclear trigrams: Sun — gentle, wind (above); Li — clinging, fire (below).

The message
Progress and success; firmness and correctness. The great one encounters good fortune and will not fall into error. When one speaks, the words are not heeded.

❖❖❖

(The water is beneath the marshes; everything has been drained away. Taken together, the two trigrams, indicating joyousness and danger, respectively, suggest a certain free-spirited improvisation during a time when essential resources have been exhausted. The state of affairs the hexagram describes is perilous, but the virtuous one will maintain good spirits and respond to the situation correctly.)

❖❖❖

❖ The strong is covered and obscured. Danger and joy. Who but the exemplary one faces scarcity and trial, yet continues to make progress toward the proper goal? "Firmness and correctness. The great one encounters good fortune and will not fall into error": one is strong and centrally positioned.

"When one speaks, the words are not heeded": the one who is fond of babbling is confounded.

The meaning
No water in sight; how will you deal with the problem?

The order and control that would lead to well-being is sadly lacking. You face a time of distress, opposition, and fatigue. Your first asset in dealing with such a situation is your own mindset. The hexagram places an unexpected emphasis on cheerfulness, and self-sufficiency during a time of diminished resources; if you take the time to cultivate them, these character traits will serve you well during this challenging time.

Do not be surprised to find that others greet your efforts with misunderstanding our outright hostility. A necessary sacrifice on your part is a real possibility. Maintain self-discipline, forbearance, and a sense of humor, and the situation will gradually improve. In the end, your commitment to reaching your goal will pay off. However you are pressured, you must remain the master of yourself, and pursue the proper, noble aim you have settled on.

One hazards one's life in pursuit of the aim one has selected.

Key concepts:
Marshes; water; scarcity; trial; self-discipline; opposition; endurance.

Hexagram Forty-eight: Ching
The well

Primary trigrams: K'an — abysmal, water (upper); Sun — gentle, wind (lower).
Nuclear trigrams: Li — clinging, fire (above); Tui — delighted, marshes (below).

The message

A town may be changed, but its well will remain the same. No reduction, no increase; those who come and go can draw out and enjoy its benefits. If, however, one is about to withdraw from the well, and the rope does not quite reach the water, or the bucket breaks, there is misfortune.

❖❖❖

(Sun signifies not only wind, but also wood. This leads to the image of water above wood: the water-wheel or pulley holding a bucket, which descends into the mouth of the underground spring and brings the water up to the top. Notions of shared resources, and the appropriate maintenance of community assets, occupy this hexagram. Access to the town well carried immense implications for the stability and well-being of agrarian villages; the symbol serves here as a metaphor for sound spiritual values and virtue in one's governing style.)

❖❖❖

❖ Wood in the water and the raising of the water; this is a well. A well supplies nourishment without becoming exhausted.
   "A town may be changed, but its well will remain the same": a central location is combined with strength.

The meaning

The town well occupied the central position in an arrangement we would recognize as a tic-tac-toe grid; the eight surrounding plots of land were developed by the eight families settling the area, and all were responsible for maintaining the common water supply. Just as this well holds its central location, so your character must establish a deep foundation. You must strive to develop what one of the parables of Jesus refers to as "root" in yourself, and then you will be in a position to undertake positive action for the larger community . . . to nourish that community, if you will.

   Time and place may alter, but the general principle for harmonious dealings with others remain the same: Authority must be exercised in the pursuit of the nourishment of the community. If you bear this in mind, you will have success. If you don't, you will shatter your bucket and encounter misfortune.

THANKS.

Key concepts:
Water; wood; community; propriety; order;
commonality; nourishment.

Hexagram Forty-nine: Ko
Shedding old skin

Primary trigrams: Tui — delighted, marshes (upper); Li — clinging, fire (lower).

Nuclear trigrams: Ch'ien — creative, heaven (above); Sun — gentle, wind (below).

The message

Only when something has been accomplished is one believed. There will be great progress and success. Advantage will come from being firm and correct, and in such a case the occasion for repentance will disappear.

❖❖❖

(Fire [the lower trigram] within the marshlands [the upper trigram] means great change is at hand. The fire makes the waters evaporate; the water extinguishes the flames. The Li trigram indicates clarity and intelligence; the Tui trigram, joy. Neither suggests random, haphazard rebelliousness. The image of molting appealed to in the hexagram's name points toward a change that has been duly prepared for, one that is wholly in keeping with the natural order of things.)

❖❖❖

❖ Water and fire extinguish each other; two daughters live together, but with their minds directed to different aims. This is called revolution. "Only when something has been accomplished is one believed": when one succeeds in making revolutionary change, one finds faith is accorded. Intelligence and joy: "great progress and success" by means of what is correct. When revolution takes place in the proper way, "occasion for repentance will disappear."

Heaven and earth undergo their changes, and the four seasons complete their functions.

The meaning

Change is either taking place, or in order, in your affairs. This change may be quite dramatic, but it is nevertheless necessary. Let the old be replaced by the new, but remember, too, that you can't expect to rip the skin from the snake before its time has come. If you must work with others in executing a new plan, be sure to do so with as much clarity, intelligence, and optimism as you can manage. You will need to win support, even for an undertaking that may seem to carry obvious benefits.

Don't let the task of finding a new way of doing things lead you to indulge in any excess or loss of perspective. Change may be necessary to replace something that has fallen into stagnation and decay, but change without a definite sense of purpose is dangerous. Be sure what you are about to undertake is necessary and appropriate to the time. Maintain a firmly virtuous mindset in dealing with new situations as they arise. Do not act selfishly.

The exemplary one puts the calendar into its correct pattern, and makes clear the seasons and the times.

I'VE GOT HALF A MIND TO POLISH OFF THAT DESIGN FOR A CHAINSAW I WAS WORKING ON LAST WEEK...

Key concepts:
Marshes; fire; change; progression; appropriateness; preparation; renovation; reform.

Hexagram Fifty: Ting
The caldron

Primary trigrams: Li — clinging, fire (upper); Sun — gentle, wind.
Nuclear trigrams: Tui — delighted, marshes (above); Ch'ien — creative, heaven (below).

The message
Great progress and success.

❖❖❖

(The upper trigram represents fire; the lower, in addition to wind, represents wood. The image of wood below and fire above calls to mind the fire prepared for a sacrificial vessel. The physical structure of the hexagram also suggests a caldron, with the bottom line seen as the legs, the three solid [yang] lines above it the body of the caldron, the next line the two "ears," and the topmost line the cover.)

❖❖❖

❖ The image is that of a caldron. Wood penetrates fire, which presents the idea of cooking. Holy people cooked their offerings in order to present them to God, and made great feasts to nourish the wise and able.

Gentleness and obedience lead to ears quick of hearing and eyes clear-sighted. The weak is advanced and acts above, in the central place, and is responded to by the strong.

All these things suggest "great progress and success."

The meaning
The caldron has to do with cooking, piety, and the nourishment of others; if you follow this hexagram's suggestion, you will use the resources available to you to offer protection, encouragement, and support to the people of wisdom and ability who are in your circle. You will also keep an open mind to the new ideas suggested by those you support.

Maintain correct relationships with those who are influential, wise, or gifted, and you will not regret it. The development of stable, secure alliances with those who can aid your cause is in order.

By the same token, you may find that a superior extends a welcome invitation to you to join a select group. Be sure that you observe all the proprieties in assuming the new place that has been made for you, and you will be able to make progress toward a worthy goal.

Key concepts:
Fire; wood; order; stability; alliances;
nourishment.

Hexagram Fifty-one: Chen
Thunder

Primary trigrams: Chen — arousing, thunder (upper); Chen — arousing, thunder (lower).
Nuclear trigrams: K'an — abysmal, water (above); Ken — unmoving, the mountain (below).

The message
Ease and expansion. Thunder comes: apprehension! Yet there is one who smiles and talks cheerfully. When the thunder terrifies everyone within a hundred miles, the one who holds the ladle and the sacrificial chalice will not drop them.

❖❖❖

(Thunder above thunder: a resounding peal! The Chen hexagram signifies, among other things, rousing and movement. Its double appearance here indicates a particularly loud sudden outburst or sharp motion. The hexagram deals with the proper reaction during times of change and shock.)

❖❖❖

❖ "Thunder comes: apprehension!": Dread is followed by happiness. "Yet there is one who smiles and talks cheerfully": Now there is a rule for one to follow. "The shock terrifies everyone within a hundred miles":
It startles the distant and frightens the near.

The meaning
Movement and action, sudden and powerful. You must be aware of the dangers of the time, and take appropriate precautions. By maintaining the correct path and seeing to it that you instill in yourself the proper regulation and self-discipline, you will be in a good position to overcome any problems and attain your goal.

You must be superior to the forces that confront you, and never lose your sense of purpose. Set about the virtuous action you are called upon to undertake. In responding to movement and advancement, you move and advance in your own disciplined way, having overcome fear and hesitation. If you are truly the master of yourself, you will be the master of the turbulent — and promising — situation at hand.

The exemplary one begins in fear and apprehension to review what has passed in life so far, and sets about a course of self-examination.

HALFWAY THERE...

Key concepts:
Thunder; surprise; poise; movement;
expansion; beginnings.

Hexagram Fifty-two: Ken
Stillness, the mountain

Primary trigrams: Ken — unmoving, the mountain (upper); Ken — unmoving, the mountain (lower).
Nuclear trigrams: Chen — arousing, thunder (above); K'an — abysmal, water (below).

The message
When one's back is at rest, one loses all consciousness of self. One walks in the courtyard, and does not see anyone there. No error.

❖❖❖

(The trigram representing a mountain is here repeated in both the upper and lower positions. Keeping one's back still is the first step towed a poise and resolve reminiscent of a mountain. Although the attribute attributed to the mountain is stillness, it would be a mistake to view this hexagram as a injunction to observe complete passivity. A mountain both rests on the surface of the earth and rises up from it; it is also an obstacle that stops travelers from moving forward.)

❖❖❖

❖ Stillness denotes stopping or resting. One rests when it is time to rest, and acts when it is time to act. When one's movements and restings all take place at the proper time, one's way is brilliant and clear.

Resting in one's resting-point means resting in one's proper place. The upper and lower correspond exactly with one another; this is why it is said, "One loses all consciousness of self. One walks in the courtyard, and does not see anyone there. No error."

The meaning
A mountain occupies exactly the position it should; any other place for it is unthinkable. Similarly, you must rest in that which is right on the very widest scale. Hold fast to enduring principles, and plan your next move accordingly. Maintain firm convictions at all costs, and choose your moment wisely. Do not become distracted with thoughts of personal gain. Instead, study your surroundings with great care. Focus properly and intently on the situation at hand, and limit yourself to that which is appropriate to your position. You will find the correct way. It may be action, inaction, or an intriguing hybrid of the two.

There is a Zen story of a man who was sent by his kinsmen to upbraid a young relative for squandering the family fortune. He reached the house and, because the young man loved him dearly, was welcomed in enthusiastically. The older man said nothing of his mission the first day. On the morning of the second, he asked his young kinsman to help him tie the strap of his sandal. "I am getting old now," he remarked, "and I suppose I will need such assistance more and more." The hint was enough; the young man mended his ways.

Key concepts:
Mountains; stillness; correct action;
observation; appropriate limitation of activity.

Hexagram Fifty-three: Chien
Gradually progressing

Primary trigrams: Sun — gentle, wind (upper); Ken — unmoving, the mountain (lower).
Nuclear trigrams: Li — clinging, fire (above); K'an — abysmal, water (below).

The message
The maiden enters into marriage: good fortune. There will be advantage in being firm and correct.

❖❖❖

(In addition to representing wind, the upper trigram Sun also signifies wood. The image is that of a tree atop a mountain. A tree grows slowly, enriching its environment as it does so. The reference to a maiden entering into marriage provides an example of an important event that is best approached by means of a series of intermediate steps. Marrying very recent acquaintances on the spur of the moment has its drawbacks.)

❖❖❖

❖ The advances indicated by gradual progress are seen in the good fortune attending the marriage of the maiden. Advancing, attaining the correct place: This indicates the achievements of successful progress. The advance is made according to correctness — in this way one rectifies one's country. The place is strong, and the center is attained.

In stillness and penetration, we see a movement that cannot be exhausted.

The meaning
The tree grows slowly at the peak of the mountain, and its shade extends as it does so. Similarly, you must make slow, steady progress toward the goal of improving yourself and making a positive impact on others.

Progression toward a goal is often best accomplished through a series of gradual, successive efforts. In this way a sound example is provided for everyone, no important steps are skipped, and the attainment of your objective is all the sweeter at the end.

You will make progress toward your goal, but you should always remember that it is best to do so by proceeding in a way that is both orderly and correct. This holds true in the attainment of responsibility and rank, and in many other things as well. Bearing this in mind, you should avoid any impetuous or ill-conceived action. With moral strength, commitment, and diligence, you will improve both yourself and those around you.

Stay the course, work on yourself, and do not demand instant results. In the end, continuous self-improvement is the same thing as continuous progress toward a worthy goal that enriches the greater community.

Key concepts:
Wood; the mountain; patience; order; steady
advancement; deliberation.

Hexagram Fifty-four: Kuei Mei

The younger maiden marries

Primary trigrams: Chen — arousing, thunder (upper); Tui — delighted, marshes (lower).
Nuclear trigrams: K'an — abysmal, water (above); Li — clinging, fire (below).

The message
The action leads to misfortune. Nothing in the least advantageous.

❖❖❖

(In addition to representing thunder over the marshes — a sign of autumnal decline — the two trigrams depict the eldest son and the youngest daughter, respectively. The resulting hexagram presents a marriage in which a young daughter marries of her own volition, and before her elder sister — acts which were considered serious, and socially destabilizing, breaches of propriety. Adding to the hexagram's note of disapproval was the taboo against younger-woman/older-man marriages; these were considered licentious and unsound. A complex, inauspicious hexagram about the passing of workable social and political arrangements. It hints at endings and beginnings of nearly cosmic scale.)

❖❖❖

❖ We see the great and righteous relation between heaven and earth; if heaven and earth have no contact with one another, things decline and fail to flourish. Satisfaction and movement: it is the youngest girl who marries. "The action leads to misfortune": Things are not in their appropriate places.

"Nothing in the least advantageous": The weak are mounted upon the strong.

The meaning
Autumn sets in, and you are reminded of the transitoriness of all things. The present situation may force you to encounter decay, corruption, or scandal. Dealings with others will very likely be marked with hardship and misunderstanding, and there is a real possibility of deterioration in previously ordered relationships. You may encounter loss and tumult.

At a time when moral codes are ignored, personal or professional associations are shattered, and painful actions are undertaken heedlessly, it is hard to recall that even in disharmony there is harmony. But you will gain some comfort if you remind yourself of this. The current cycle must play itself through, and the abuses of the times must be endured. Near the end of *King Lear*, Shakespeare has Edgar say to his blinded father, "What? In ill thoughts again? Men must endure their going hence even as their coming hither." Adopting this attitude of enlightened acceptance of the comings and goings of human systems — and, indeed, of humanity — is the advice offered by this difficult hexagram.

The exemplary one is not deceived by that which is transitory, but rather focuses on the ultimate end.

GEE, IT SEEMED LIKE SUCH A GOOD IDEA AT THE TIME....

Key concepts:
Thunder; marshes; autumn; decay; renewal; transitoriness.

133

Hexagram Fifty-five: Feng

Abundance

Primary trigrams: Chen — arousing, thunder (upper); Li — clinging, fire (lower).
Nuclear trigrams: Tui — delighted, marshes (above); Sun — gentle, wind (below).

The message
Progress and development. When a king has reached the point of abundance, there is no reason for anxiety. He should be like the sun at noontime.

❖❖❖

(Chen, thunder, is above Li, here interpreted as lightning. Together, the trigrams yield the unmistakable image of a thunderstorm that clears the air with great power and authority. Such power takes the form of movement that is clear and brilliant; this supports the idea of fullness , abundance, and the overcoming of all hindrances. But even such power does not endure unchanged.)

❖❖❖

❖ Abundance denotes greatness. Brilliance, and movement directed by that brilliance. This is abundance. "A king has reached the point of abundance": One must incline toward greatness. "There is no reason for anxiety. He should be like the sun at noontime": One illuminates the whole world. The sun no sooner stands at its highest point but it begins to decline. The moon no sooner becomes full but it begins to wane.

Heaven and earth, then, provide vigor and abundance, and thereafter dullness and want, according to the seasons. How much more must it be so among humans? How much more must it be so in the spiritual realm?

The meaning
The power of a thunderstorm is at your disposal: make the most of it. Act judiciously, resolve outstanding disputes, and set about the business of prosperous activity. The good times before you will not last forever.

Preserving a state of prosperity can be a difficult undertaking. Keen intelligence and the willingness to take decisive action will be necessary if you are to extend the good times before you. if you can incorporate these two virtues in your affairs, you stand a good chance of consolidating your position and enjoying your bounty for a longer period than you would have otherwise.

In your interactions with others, you should be sure to demonstrate the positive outlook appropriate to a time of abundance. Do not make the mistake of seeing each new and profitable undertaking only as a new collection of worries. When you find that you can put your mind to nearly anything and accomplish it, you should enjoy yourself.

Key concepts:
Thunder; lightning; power; plenty; judicious
action; opportunity.

Hexagram Fifty-six: Lu
The traveler abroad

Primary trigrams: Li — clinging, fire (upper); Ken — unmoving, the mountain (lower).
Nuclear trigrams: Tui — delighted, marshes (above); Sun — gentle, wind (below).

The message
There may be some small attainment and progress. If the traveler is firm and correct, as is required, there will be good fortune.

❖❖❖

(Fire burns on the mountain; although the mountain is stationary, the fire moves about aimlessly. This suggests the image of a traveler, the so-called "stranger in a strange land." The directions associated with the two trigrams are opposite: fire rises upward, and the mountain pushes downward. The contact between the two is not an enduring one.)

❖❖❖

❖ "There may be some small attainment and progress": The weak occupies the central place in the outer region, and is obedient to the strong. Stillness and an adherence to clarity; this is why it is said, "There may be some small attainment and progress. If the traveler is firm and correct, as is required, there will be good fortune."

Great is the right course to be taken in the time of the wanderer.

The meaning
A roving fire at the peak of the mountain; you should not expect long-term commitments or rewards, as such fires usually extinguish themselves in short order. Through humility and integrity you may expect to avoid injury and make modest progress toward your goal, but you are not likely to find a permanent place for yourself in the current state of affairs.

Restraint is in order. You should cultivate an inner strength that will see you through the time, and be content to make humble advancement toward your goal for a certain period. Rash or combative undertakings will not succeed.

Do not struggle with feelings of alienation and rootlessness. Instead, you should try to instill in yourself docility, intelligence, restfulness, and an appreciation of solitude. These virtues will serve to smooth the sometimes difficult path you will walk as an outsider. In *Medea*, Euripides writes, "It is right for foreigners to adapt to the prevailing customs; for my part, I say there is no excuse in offending one's neighbors through pride and ill manners." The humility that these lines appeal to (at least on the surface), as well as the inner reserve necessary to cultivate that humility, point toward the virtues this hexagram promotes.

Key concepts:
Fire; the mountain; restraint; exclusion;
drifting; humility.

Hexagram Fifty-seven: Sun
Wind, penetration

Primary trigrams: Sun — gentle, wind (upper); Sun — gentle, wind (lower).

Nuclear trigrams: Li — clinging, fire (above); Tui — delighted, marshes (below).

The message

There will be some little attainment and progress. There will be advantage in movement in any direction whatsoever. It will be advantageous to see the great man.

❖❖❖

(The Sun trigram represents both wind and wood; among its attributes are gentleness and penetration. It appears in both the upper and lower positions here; the topic of the hexagram is obedience to the will of a superior, which influences others as a strong wind does a blade of grass.)

❖❖❖

❖ The gentle, doubled; the orders are repeated. The strong has penetrated into the central and correct place, and the will is carried into effect The weak lines are obedient to the strong. This is why it is said, "There will be some little attainment and progress. There will be advantage in movement in any direction whatsoever. It will be advantageous to see the great man."

The meaning

The wind blows everywhere, persistently, and in this way exercises its influence; so it is with worthy initiatives if you want them to be carried out properly. You may need to repeat instructions in order to attain your goal.

If there is a problem that you must resolve, you will need to win the help of others in overcoming it. To be effective, orders must penetrate the consciousness of your subordinates fully if you expect to get the results you are after. Admittedly, this is not always the easiest thing to accomplish, but if you are not speaking in a language that will be understood by others, there is no point blaming anyone other than yourself for the deadlock that results. The assistance of an elder or esteemed associate may be in order. Calling attention to yourself, or appealing to your own authority, is not likely to yield good results.

Be sure the message you intend to send is the one that is being received. With proper communication and the recruitment of assistance where it is needed, you may expect to make modest progress. This hexagram emphasizes both repetitiveness (when necessary) and a certain subtlety in one's dealings with others. It is a reminder that communications with subordinates must be intelligently delivered, and that instructions received from a superior must be faithfully carried out.

The exemplary one reiterates his orders, and so secures the endeavor.

OKAY, ALREADY, I GET IT, I GET IT...

Key concepts:
Wind; repetition; penetration; communication; authority; subtlety; harmony; obedience.

Hexagram Fifty-eight: Tui

The delighted, marshes

Primary trigrams: Tui — delighted, marshes (upper); Tui — delighted, marshes (lower).
Nuclear trigrams: Sun — gentle, wind (above); Li — clinging, fire (below).

The message

There will be progress and attainment. It will be advantageous to be firm and correct.

❖❖❖

(The trigram Tui, which appears here in both the upper and lower positions, symbolizes water as collected in a marsh or lake. Its most prominent feature is pleasure or complacent satisfaction. The hexagram is concerned with the serene form of happiness that gives rise to both a sense of personal wholeness and correct dealings with others..)

❖❖❖

❖ The delighted denotes pleased satisfaction. The strong in the center, and the weak on the outward part; in pleasure what is most advantageous is the maintenance of firm correctness. Through this there will be found an accordance with heaven, and harmony with men. When pleasure such as this is what leads the people, they forget their toils; when it helps them to confront difficulties, they forget death.

How great is the power of the delighted, which so inspires the people!

The meaning

Delight follows delight. Even if mildness and harmony prevail in your nature, they must be directed by true-heartedness, and the integrity to control and direct them. This is true pleasure, which you should not confuse with indulgence for the sake of personal gratification.

In your dealings with others, show gentleness, sincerity, and modesty. Cast aside worries and anxieties, and do your very best to understand the problems of other people. If you do all this with joy, you will be in an excellent position to overcome any obstacle that may come your way.

This hexagram, although it is generally auspicious, is not a guarantee against the appearance of adversity. It is a reminder that the ability to overcome anxiety, to undertake the conscious cultivation of joy in one's life, is one of the most distinctive — and glorious — parts of being human. Its advice parallels that of the Christian Bible: "Therefore take no thought, saying, What shall we eat? or, What shall we drink? or, Wherewithal shall we be clothed? For after all these things do the Gentiles seek. For your heavenly father knoweth that ye have need of all these things. But seek ye first the kingdom of God, and his righteousness."

Key concepts:
Marshes; serenity; contentment; satisfaction;
freedom from anxiety and doubt.

Hexagram Fifty-nine: Huan
Dissipation

Primary trigrams: Sun — gentle, wind (upper); K'an — abysmal, water (lower).
Nuclear trigrams: Ken — unmoving, the mountain (above); Chen — arousing (below).

The message
There will be progress and success. The king goes to his ancestral temple; it will be advantageous to cross the great stream. It will be advantageous to be firm and correct.

❖❖❖

(Wind above the water; the water ripples and scatters. This hexagram warns against the "ripple effect" that occurs when one's mind deviates, or the minds of others deviate, from the right course. Precautions against such divisive, chaotic influences are offered: order is to be maintained through correct perseverance. The upper trigram signifies not only wind, but also wood, which here suggests the boat one uses to "cross the great stream" — undertake an important task.)

❖❖❖

❖ "There will be progress and success": the strong is below, and suffers no extinction; the weak occupies its place in the outer realm, and unites with that which is above. "The king goes to his ancestral temple": His mind is without any deflection.

"It will be advantageous to cross the great stream": one rides in a vessel of wood, and one does so with success.

The meaning
The wind blows and the water scatters — but if you maintain a mind that is clear, ready, and open, like the king who returns to his ancestral temple, you will weather the storm. Follow what is right, and reinforce it in your heart, and you will be able to overcome potentially divisive influences.

If the situation demands commitment to a great or hazardous effort, you should undertake it. But remember that your every action must be executed with due attention to what is morally sound, and with both firmness and correctness.

The Tao Te Ching remarks, in a similar vein, on potentially chaotic situations that are calmed by means of adherence to uprightness: "When the great Way was forsaken, there was humaneness and righteous action."

Key concepts:
Wind; water; division; piety; righteousness;
order; correct action.

Hexagram Sixty: Chieh
Limitation

Primary trigrams: K'an — abysmal, water (upper); Tui — delighted, marshes (lower).

Nuclear trigrams: Ken — unmoving, the mountain (above); Chen — arousing, thunder (below).

The message
There will be progress and attainment. If the limitations are severe and difficult, they should not be made permanent.

❖❖❖

(Water above marshes; if the marsh receives too much water, it will overflow, but if it does not receive enough, it will run dry. The idea of the hexagram is that of regulation, restraint, and regular division; the lines of Chieh are compared to the pattern of the recurring joints of a bamboo stalk, a correlation that strengthens the notion of repetitive regulation and restraint. The subject of the hexagram is the proper exercise of regulatory authority in dealing with others and distributing resources.)

❖❖❖

❖ "Progress and attainment": The strong and weak are divided equally, and the strong occupies the central positions. "If the limitations are severe and difficult, they should not be made permanent": Such a course would lead to the end of the matter. Pleasure and satisfaction directing the course amidst peril: all regulations controlled, and in the proper place. Free action proceeds from the central and correct position. Heaven and earth observe their regular terms, and we have the four seasons complete.

When one frames measures according to the correct regulation, the resources suffer no injury, and the people are not abused.

The meaning
When the water pours into the marsh without extremity, the situation is correct; similarly, the constraints you set on others in your dealings with them must not be extreme, but appropriate to the situation. The same is true of the decisions you make in allocating resources.

The rules you enact, and the order you establish, must be adapted to circumstances, rather than applied blindly without regard to the facts. Act moderately and prudently, and do not fall into the trap of going "by the book" in order to avoid thinking in the first place. If you can institute sensible, moderate guidance in the standards you set down, you can expect to encounter success. If, on the other hand, you assume that the simple issuing of a familiar command is sufficient to any situation, you will quickly learn an expensive lesson about the nature of leadership.

Exercise moderation and sound judgment in your interactions with others, and you will make progress.

Key concepts:
Water; marshes; regulation; proper restraint;
moderation; time; regular division.

Hexagram Sixty-one: Chung Fu

The truth within

Primary trigrams: Sun — gentle, wind (upper); Tui — delighted, marshes (lower).
Nuclear trigrams: Ken — unmoving, the mountain (above); Chen — arousing, thunder(below).

The message

The truth within moves even pigs and fish, and leads to good fortune. There will be advantage in crossing the great stream. There will be advantage in being firm and correct.

❖❖❖

(A marsh, and the wind above it; wind penetrates everywhere, and reinvigorates the collected waters of the marsh. Even secret and enclosed things are penetrated by its force. The wind is compared in this hexagram to the pervasive nature of perfect sincerity and truth. The reference to "pigs and fishes" suggests that such truth animates even the lowly. The association of sublime truth with emptiness — rendered by the two broken [yin] lines in the center — is worth noting. The Sun trigram represents not only wind, but also wood, and here suggests a special "empty" boat for the purpose of "crossing the great stream": undertaking an important task.)

❖❖❖

❖ Weakness in the interior, strength in the central places. Pleased satisfaction and flexible penetration. The truth within will transform a country. "Pigs and fish; there will be good fortune": Innermost truth reaches even to pigs and fishes. "There will be advantage in crossing the great stream": One rides on wood, which forms an empty boat.

In innermost truth, "there will be advantage in being firm and correct." In that virtue indeed we have a response to heaven.

The meaning

The wind of truth transforms everything and resolves every imaginable flaw; if you cultivate your inner self, you will succeed in the most difficult undertakings. Is an important task waiting to be performed? You should rise to the occasion and perform it with all due discipline and virtue.

In the final analysis, you will not earn any dominance over others by acting in accordance with the innermost truth described in this auspicious hexagram. To the contrary, you will free yourself from all preoccupation with the very notion of self. You will cultivate solid, unshakable virtue and move ahead humbly.

The Buddhists say, "Even the Buddha is constantly working on himself." The injunction here to tap into resources of sublime influence, yet retain the humble "advantage of being firm and correct," is not far off in spirit.

The exemplary one wants to discuss the causes of litigation, and delays the imposition of a death sentence.

OM.

Key concepts:
Wind; marshes; truth; transformation; flawlessness; deliberation; wisdom; humility.

Hexagram Sixty-two: Hsiao Kuo

Exceeding in what is small

Primary trigrams: Chen — arousing, thunder (upper); Ken — unmoving, the mountain (lower).
Nuclear trigrams: Tui — delighted, low-lying waters (above); Sun — gentle, wind (below).

The message

There will be progress and attainment. But it will be advantageous to be firm and correct. Efforts in small affairs are advised. Efforts in large affairs are not advised. The notes of the bird on the wing descend, and it is better to descend than to rise up. There will be great good fortune.

❖❖❖

(Thunder above the mountain; the sound issues forth with great power, but recedes as it travels. The hexagram discusses modesty in ambition, general forbearance, and the wisdom of knowing when not to attempt to change a situation dramatically. The discussion of the bird is inspired by the physical structure of the hexagram; the top two and bottom two lines are seen as wings. The remarks on this bird are intended to show the virtue of humility: it is to the bird's advantage to descend while a branch is within reach, rather than soar into inhospitable regions.)

❖❖❖

The small exceed the rest. Progress and attainment. Such exceeding, in order to be advantageous, must be firm and correct. That is, it must take place according to the requirements of the time. The weak are in central places, so it is said that "efforts in small affairs are advised." The strong is not in its proper place and is not central: "efforts in large affairs are not advised."

To ascend is unreasonable, while to descend is natural and right.

The meaning

A crack of thunder lessens in force, almost as if it knows that the time for theatrics has passed. Similarly, you should scale back your expectations and seek advantage only in appropriate circumstances.

You may find yourself asking, "Is it ever appropriate to change from the course that's been established as correct?" In the current state of affairs, the answer is "no" when dealing with fundamental issues of right and wrong, but "yes" when the change of course affects only external or seemingly superficial matters. In fact, making such a change in form or appearance is extremely beneficial just now. Change the form, but not the substance, of a worthy undertaking. If you show care, humility, and a certain healthy respect for the essentials of things, you may expect significant success. Great benefit may arise from your attempts to make changes that appear modest or even cosmetic in nature. A top-to-bottom overhaul is not what is required in the current situation; think instead in terms of a single deft twist of one small screw.

Key concepts:
Thunder; the mountain; appropriateness;
humility; discretion.

Hexagram Sixty-three:
Chi Chi

Having crossed the stream

Primary trigrams: K'an — abysmal, water (upper); Li — clinging, fire (lower).
Nuclear trigrams: Li — clinging, fire (above); K'an — abysmal, water (below).

The message
Progress and success in small matters. There will be advantage in being firm and correct. There has been good fortune in the beginning; there may be disorder in the end.

❖❖❖

(Water suspended above a fire. If the water is released, it douses the fire; if the flames get too hot and rise too high, the water will be evaporated. As it stands, however, the elements occupy their places properly; note the symmetrical inversion of the nuclear trigrams. While the upper primary trigram carries the meaning of danger; the lower suggests intelligence and foresight. Broken [yin] and solid [yang] lines alternate appropriately. "Having crossed the stream" refers to the period after a trying, but successful, undertaking. The situation is one of harmony and completion that nevertheless demands some consolidating measures.)

❖❖❖

❖ "Progress and success." The success comes in small matters. "There will be advantage in being firm and correct": The strong and weak are correctly arranged, with appropriate placement. "There has been good fortune in the beginning": The weak is in the center.

If one stops at the end, disorder results, and the course is at an end.

The meaning
Fire and water in balance, but they must still be tended closely. After working hard to achieve balance and harmony, you may be tempted to withdraw and let matters sort themselves out on their own. This would be a mistake.

This is not a time for drastic changes in the arrangement of things; there is, after all, a general balance to what you have established. But something remains to be done. Small measures must be undertaken to consolidate the gains inherent in the situation at hand. Without noise or commotion, you must go on, with firm correctness, to complete what has been accomplished, bearing in mind the inherent instability of every human undertaking.

By means of subtle action, you should refine and develop that which has been enacted. Then you will enjoy the full benefit of your attainment. After it has reached its peak, however, a decline is inevitable.

The exemplary one thinks about misfortunes that may arise, and guards against them beforehand.

Key concepts:
Fire; water; balance; imbalance; caution;
prudence; consolidation.

Hexagram Sixty-four: Wei Chi

Having not yet crossed the stream

Primary trigrams: Li — clinging, fire (upper); K'an — abysmal, water (lower).
Nuclear trigrams: K'an — abysmal, water (above); Li — clinging, fire (below).

The message

Progress and success. Yet for a young fox that has nearly crossed, but has immersed his tail in the water, there will be no advantage in any way.

❖❖❖

(Fire above water. Fire burns upward, water flows downward. The two are not in harmony and cannot affect one another. The hexagram suggests profoundly disparate forces arrayed in an uncomplimentary manner. If one expects to create order from such a situation, great caution and discipline are in order. "Having not yet crossed the stream" means that the great undertaking has not yet been accomplished. The brash young fox tries, but fails, to make a dash across the stream by jumping along chunks of ice. Anyone watching from the bank would be reminded of the folly of relying too much on one's own strength.)

❖❖❖

❖ "Progress and success": The weak is in the center. "The young fox has nearly crossed the stream," but he hasn't escaped what's in the middle. His tail is immersed, and "there will be no advantage in any way": The end does not carry through the beginning.

Although the places are not appropriate, the strong and the weak are in correspondence.

The meaning

Fire and water in conflict; the time of order in your situation has ended, and you must begin the struggle for coherence once again.

This is a fine message for a supposedly auspicious hexagram! But disorder is to be expected in human affairs, and the ability to react to it properly is an advantage you should not underestimate. Knowing the difference between polar opposites may seem to be child's play, but it is often the work of a lifetime. Look closely at the true nature of that which is presented in the current situation; be sure that you are not expecting inappropriate results.

Do not imagine that strength, cunning, or impulsiveness masquerading as bravado will be sufficient to bring about completion of the task. Be careful. Do your utmost to promote harmony in your relationships with others; there is probably work waiting for you on this front. A situation that is in a condition of apparently complete disorder can be turned toward order by humble effort and continuous correct action. This kind of action should be your objective.

The exemplary one knows the difference between one thing and another, and understands where things should go.

YOU KNOW, THIS JUST MIGHT GET TRICKY...

Key concepts:
Fire; water; disharmony; incoherence; lack of order; caution; prudence.

Bibliography

Of the books listed below, the translation by Richard Wilhelm and Cary F. Baynes is the most acclaimed modern rendering of the *I Ching*. The Wilhelm/Baynes translation is an excellent next step for those who are interested in deeper studies of the oracle than this book undertakes. So is James Legge's inspired (and highly influential) translation of 1899, although some may find it challenging in places.

Blofield, John. *The Book of Change: A New Translation of the Ancient Chinese I Ching (Yi-King)*. London: Allen and Unwin, 1965. New York: E.P. Dutton, 1968.

Legge, James, translator. *The Yi-King*, part two of *The Sacred Books of China: The Texts of Confucianism*. Sacred Books of the East, edited by F. Max Muller, vol. 16. Oxford: Clarendon, 1882. Second edition, 1899. (The second edition is available in an unaltered reissue from Dover Publications, New York.)

Melyan, Gary, and Chu, Wen-kuang. *The Pocket I Ching*. Tokyo: Charles E. Tuttle Company, Inc. 1977.

Van Over, Raymond, ed. *I Ching*. New York: Mentor Books, New American Library, 1971.

Wilhelm, Richard, and Baynes, C.F., translators. *The I Ching or Book of Changes*. Bollingen Series 19. Princeton: Princeton University Press. Third edition, 1961.